HEBREW BULLAE FROM THE TIME OF JEREMIAH

Nahman Avigad

HEBREW BULLAE FROM THE TIME OF JEREMIAH

Remnants of a Burnt Archive

ISRAEL EXPLORATION SOCIETY
JERUSALEM 1986

PUBLISHED WITH THE ASSISTANCE OF
THE DOROT FOUNDATION, NEW YORK

ISBN 965-221-006-4

Translated by R. Grafman
Layout and cover – A. Pladot
Plates – Tafsar Jerusalem

PRINTED IN ISRAEL
BY BEN-ZVI PRINTING ENTERPRISES, LTD.

FROM THE COLLECTIONS OF
YOAV SASSON
THE ISRAEL MUSEUM

CONTENTS

PREFACE

The bullae published in the present study belong to the category of archaeological-epigraphical discoveries which are made accidentally but which are of prime importance for the study of ancient Israel. The most significant discovery for Bible studies in recent years, the Dead Sea Scrolls, was this very type of chance find. I was indeed fortunate in having had a part, albeit modest, in their publication shortly after their discovery. Another example is the group of Judean bullae and seals from the Persian period which I had the privilege of publishing a decade ago. And now it has fallen to my lot to study this further group of Hebrew bullae — the largest such assemblage ever found.

Few would doubt that the value of an archaeological discovery is all the greater when it originates in a controlled excavation, where the precise context of its findspot is documented. Stratigraphical excavations are often able to provide a sound chronological basis for undated epigraphical discoveries. Mere chance finds do not ordinarily enjoy such an advantage, but among this new group of Hebrew bullae there are two items which serve to provide the entire assemblage with a dating more precise than that which would derive from a normal stratigraphical context, for these bullae bear the names of personages known to us from the Bible. The obvious significance of these two bullae induced me to publish them shortly after their discovery, independent of the bulk of the group which is published here for the first time.*

It is a pleasant task to thank all those who facilitated my access to the bullae. Foremost, I am grateful to those who brought information of the discovery to my notice, immediately upon their appearance on the antiquities market; to Mr. Yoav Sasson, who purchased the major portion of the group and kindly placed it at my disposal for scrutiny; and to Dr. Reuben Hecht, who purchased a large part of the group and generously presented it to the Israel Museum in Jerusalem. (The Israel Museum, in turn, has expressed its gratitude and appreciation to Dr. Hecht for this important donation.) I am grateful to both of them, and to the Israel Museum, for granting me permission to publish the material in their possession.

Professor Benjamin Mazar has kindly read the typescript of the Hebrew version and has made valuable comments. Professor Jonas Greenfield has been helpful with his advice during my research for my corpus of Hebrew seals, of which this is a part. Z. Radovan has skilfully photographed the bullae.

It was thought advisable to accompany many of the photographs with line drawings of the bullae in which blurred and fragmentary inscriptions could be clarified;

* The present study is part of a corpus of West Semitic seals being prepared by the author, which is to be published by the Israel Academy of Sciences and Humanities. The importance and scope of the present material has led to the decision to publish it here as a separate monograph.

these also provide a graphic expression of proposed restorations. These drawings, as well as others appearing in the volume, were made by the author. All the photographs of the individual bullae are reproduced here at the scale of three times their natural size (unless otherwise stated). Damaged letters and uncertain readings have been marked in the Hebrew readings by superior dots; restored letters are contained within square brackets.

I must thank Mr. R. Grafman, the translator, who also skilfully rendered my publication of the previous group of bullae into English; to Mrs. Sue Gorodetsky for editing the English text; and to Abraham Pladot for the layout of the book. Finally, I wish to express my gratitude to Mr. Joseph Aviram for his part in expediting the publication of this volume in exemplary fashion.

N. Avigad

1. INTRODUCTION

Research into seals of the biblical period has recently gained impetus from the unexpected discovery of several large assemblages of bullae bearing Hebrew inscriptions. A bulla is formed by impressing a seal on a small lump of clay attached to a written document; thus, it inherently contains somewhat more information than the seal itself. Not many years ago the known Hebrew bullae could still be counted on the fingers of one hand. However, with the sharp increase in the number of known seals and bullae, and advances in modern research into them, their full historical and cultural value is emerging.

The new discovery which is the subject of this study represents a most significant innovation, since for the first time two individuals who left their mark on bullae may be identified with characters mentioned in the Bible. When handling impressions of the personal seals of Berekhyahu/Baruch son of Neriyahu the scribe (the Prophet Jeremiah's secretary and faithful companion), or of Yerahme'el the son of the king (of whom it is related that he was sent to arrest both Jeremiah and Baruch on the order of the king), one cannot refrain from associating them with the personages who played active roles in the stormy events at the royal court prior to the fall of Jerusalem in 586 BCE.

These preliminary remarks set the scene for the period in which these bullae were originally impressed — the time of Jeremiah. The bullae themselves bear only the names of persons and in several cases their titles, but there is no indication of the circumstances in which they were impressed. The present study primarily deals with the onomasticon of the bullae, and also discusses their use and historical significance. The author does not claim to have solved all the problems associated with the bullae, and hopes that further studies will contribute to a fuller understanding of this interesting and improtant material.

In the early 1960s, the late Y. Aharoni discovered the first group of Hebrew bullae in a pottery juglet at Lachish.[1] Of the 17 bullae, only seven were legible. This discovery led to the realization that the bullae formed part of an administrative archive at that spot, for one of them bore the title of a royal official.

In the mid-1970s, a group of almost seventy bullae and two seals from the period of the Return from Exile (the Persian period), bearing inscriptions in Aramaic script, came to light; their provenance is unknown.[2] These bullae bore the name of the province of "Yehud", and the names of officials and private individuals. The close connection between this group and the "Yehud" impressions frequently

1 Y. Aharoni: *Investigations at Lachish: The Sanctuary and Residency (Lachish V)*, Tel Aviv 1975, pp. 19–22.

2 Avigad 1976a.

found on jar handles in archaeological excavations lent additional interest to this find, providing a valuable contribution to the history of the period.

After the remarkable appearance of this second group of bullae, it seemed likely that other such discoveries would be made; there is an unwritten rule in archaeology that unique finds are generally followed by further finds of the same type. Indeed, only a year after the discovery of the Persian period bullae, a hoard of Hebrew bullae from the end of the First Temple period made its appearance — a group several times larger than the previous one. These bullae are the subject of the present monograph. The importance of this group lies not only in the large number of bullae involved, and the wide variety of types, but also in the abovementioned fact that they bear names which can be identified with certainty with known biblical individuals.

While this new group was being prepared for publication, word was received in Summer 1982 of the discovery of fifty Hebrew bullae in the City of David excavations, forty of which are legible.[3] These have been published only provisionally, but even from the preliminary treatment it is obvious that they are an important addition to the corpus of known bullae. They contain no particular new data bearing on the present study, but they are of crucial significance in that they were discovered in a controlled archaeological excavation, and in Jerusalem.

At present, since the number of Hebrew bullae has increased to such an unexpected extend, the corpus of Hebrew epigraphy in the biblical period has gained a treasure trove for onomastic and palaeographic research, material which is rich in historical, administrative, legal and social aspects. The value of this material depends on the ability of scholars to exploit to the utmost the information encapsulated in these minute documents.

A. Discovery of the Bullae

The first bullae of this group came to light in October 1975, at the shop of an antiquities dealer in Jerusalem. Further groups subsequently appeared over a period of several months. The breakdown into groups may be explained by assuming that the discoverers, Arab peasants, found them accidentally or illicitly, and that after dividing up their loot, they individually sold the portions to different antiquities dealers. Alternatively, the bullae may not all have been discovered at one time; the search for them, involving the painstaking sifting of large quantities of earth, would be a lengthy process and small quantities or bullae may have found their way to the antiquities market as they emerged.

As with any ancient object from non-controlled excavations which appears on the open antiquities market, it is impossible to ascertain the precise findspot of the bullae or the exact circumstances of their discovery. Persons who find antiquities

3 Shiloh 1984, pp. 19–20; and see now Shiloh 1985.

in this manner are rarely willing to reveal the precise source of their wares. In the present case, we were informed by the dealers that the bullae were found near Tell Beit Mirsim, in the southern Judean Shephelah. Although this information was not necessarily reliable, we immediately visited the vicinity, together with the Director of the Department of Antiquities and Museums, Avraham Eitan, and the District Archaeologist, Amos Kloner. On a hill near the mound, we did notice many traces of digging, undoubtedly left behind by illicit diggers for antiquities. However, at no point was there a sounding of adequate depth, and sufficient evidence to conclude that this was the source of the find. Nonetheless, our brief search was not very thorough, nor did it encompass the entire area where illegal digging is known to have been carried out in recent years. Thus, the matter of the exact provenance of the bullae remains unresolved.

I first received notice of the bullae through a collector of antiquities who from time to time visits the antiquities shops in Jerusalem. He brought with him the first four bullae, on which he asked my expert opinion. In a similar manner, other bullae were brought to me in small batches, and I had only a brief opportunity to examine and photograph them. There was no reason to suspect their authenticity, and I seriously doubt whether it would be possible to forge such burnt and damaged bullae. Despite the delay in the appearance of subsequent batches of bullae, there was no doubt that all of them belonged to a single assemblage; identical impressions often occurred in different batches, and occasionally two fragments of a single bullae, from different batches, could be joined. This was revealed only by means of enlarged photographs. I was never informed of the names of the antiquities dealers involved, though I was told that they were licensed Arab dealers from East Jerusalem, Bethlehem and Beit Saḥour. Only one dealer had no qualms in identifying himself — the well-known Mr. Kando who, it will be remembered, played such a key role in the episode of the Dead Sea Scrolls in 1948. However, of the entire assemblage, only eight bullae passed through his hands.

In time, the bullae changed hands among the dealers themselves. Eventually, Mr. Yoav Sasson, dealer and collector, succeeded in acquiring most of the assemblage, close to two hundred bullae, which remain in his possession. This was a most welcome development, for otherwise the bullae would have been scattered throughout the world. Dr. Reuben Hecht of Haifa purchased forty-nine further items, comprising complete bullae and fragments, and donated them to the Israel Museum in Jerusalem. The whereabouts of several bullae, not more than a dozen, cannot be traced at present, though prior to their disappearance I was able to photograph and record them. Thus, most of the bullae found are now concentrated in two major groups.

Consequently, we have been able to record essentially the entire extent of this important and impressive assemblage of sealings. Obviously, neither the dealers nor the purchasers were aware of the exact contents of the inscriptions on the bullae before my examinations. I reported to the Director of Antiquities all the events known to me in connection with the bullae, and he has taken measures to prevent their sale abroad.

obverse

A group of Bullae from the collection of Yoav Sasson

reverse

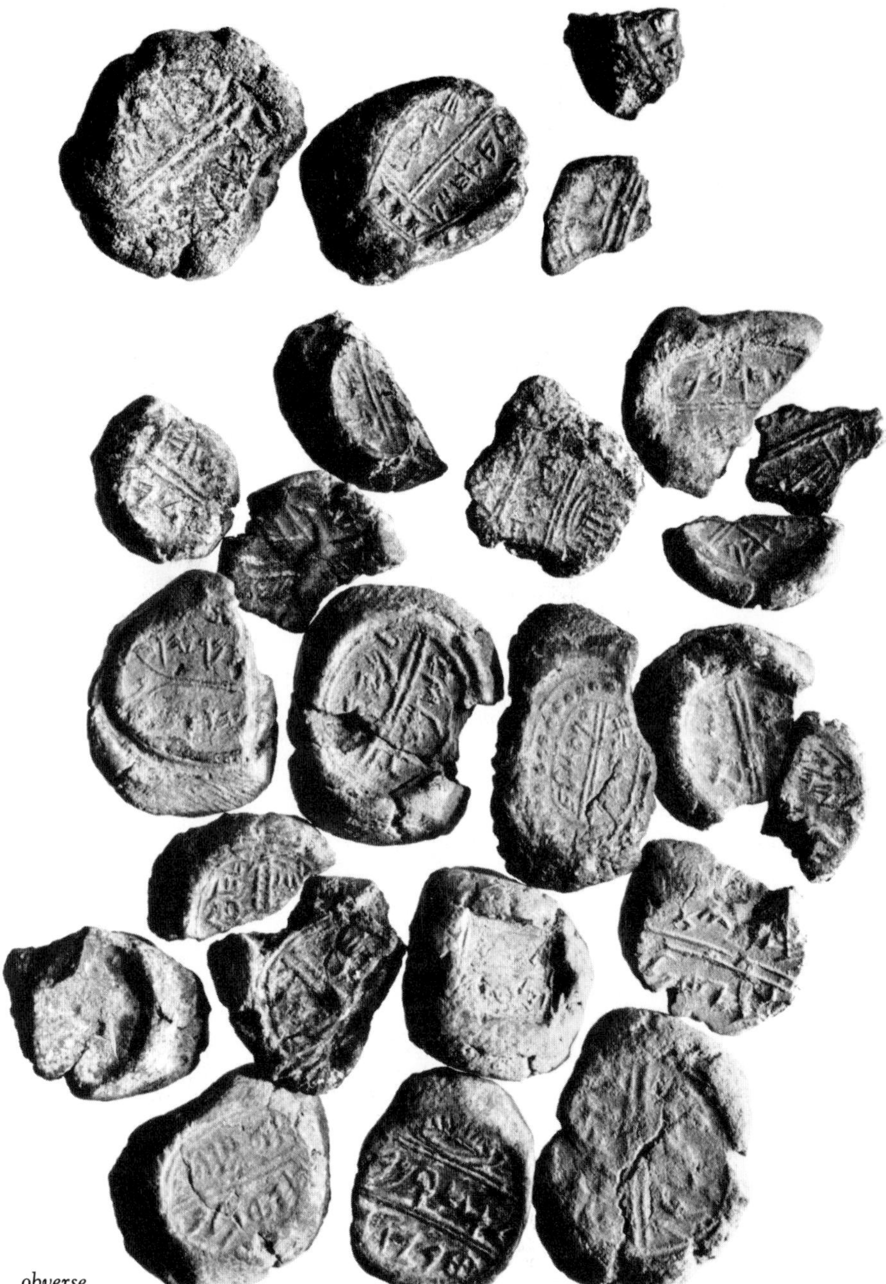

obverse

A group of Bullae from the collection of the Israel Museum

reverse

B. General Description of the Bullae

The bullae are small lumps or pieces of clay, originally attached to a string or cord which had been wound and tied around a rolled or folded papyrus scroll. The upper surface of the bullae shows the seal impressions, while on the back, impressed marks of the papyrus fibres and of the string can be discerned. Generally, the bullae are of a fine, levigated clay. Usually, the pieces of clay were deliberately formed into a uniform shape, and the seal was carefully pressed into the soft surface, resulting in a complete impression. Some bullae, however, were carelessly impressed, and the seal-impression is thus incomplete. Sometimes the clay was coarse, occasionally even with rather large grits, leading to cracks or gaps in the impression and damage to the inscription. In the margins of some of the bullae, fingerprints of the persons who impressed the seals can still be seen.

Bullae of dried clay do not generally survive in good condition in the presence of damp soil; when found in drier conditions, however, in a spot protected from penetration of moisture such as a closed vessel or a burnt stratum, they can remain intact. Many of our bullae have been preserved complete, though others are broken and damaged and of a few only small fragments remain. The assemblage clearly originates from the site of a conflagration. Though this fire destroyed the papyrus documents which had been sealed with the bullae, it baked the clay bullae themselves, making them durable. Uneven firing led to variations in the colour of the bullae, from reddish-brown through yellowish and, mainly, grey and black. Sometimes the clay was greatly overfired, making it fragile and friable.

The dimensions of the complete bullae range from 11×13 mm to 16×19 mm. The shape of the impressions of the seals is generally oval, and occasionally almost round, indicating, of course, that the seals themselves were oval; they measured from around 6×6 mm to 11×13 mm. Only one of the seals was square (No. 135), and there were two elongated ones of lentoid outline (Nos. 42 and 152). Generally, a single or double linear frame encloses the inscribed surface. This frame is often blurred, owing to the pressure of the fingers around the edges of the soft bullae. Thus, this feature is not always noted in the individual descriptions below.

The great majority of the bullae bear two-line inscriptions, with a divider in the form of two parallel lines (often close together, comprising a double line). Only rarely are the seals divided into three registers, with a two- or three-line inscription. Most of the bullae bear only inscriptions, though on a few are geometric, floral or faunal decorative motifs.

The backs of the bullae are mostly flat; occasionally they are convex, but never concave. Hence it may be assumed that the papyri to which they had been attached were not rolled as cylindrical scrolls, but rather were rolled flat or were folded. As previously noted, the backs of the bullae bear impressions of the weave of the papyrus fibres, as well as of the string which had bound the documents. Occasionally the soft clay had been pressed around the string, forming a bulla pierced along its length or width; in such cases there are no string marks on the back. The number of string impressions on each bulla ranges from one to three, showing the number of times the string had been wound around the document.

Three bullae (Nos. 6, 9 and 83) differ from the rest in that the impressions of the papyrus fibres are coarser and run in only one direction (rather than in a network). The string impressions here are curved, and the lumps of clay seem to have been applied to the loops of the knots. These grooves are especially thick and actual fibres of the string are still extant.

C. Registration of the Bullae

The entire assemblage of bullae numbers 255 items, most of them complete though some are broken; the majority are unique and others are duplicate, identical copies. The majority were impressed with seals belonging to persons who possessed only one seal, and in most cases only a single impression of each such seal was found. However, other seal-owners used their single seal more than once, and thus there are several cases of two, four and, in one instance, fourteen bullae bearing identical duplicate impressions, all sealed by a single seal. Moreover, there were other individuals who possessed two, three or as many as six different seals; all were used, and sometimes more than once. Thus, the assemblage includes duplicate bullae of multiple seals.

The bullae have been registered in the following manner: the 211 items in our register each denote a bulla or bullae impressed by a single seal; in other words, they represent 211 different *seals*, including duplicate seals. The duplicate *bullae* are denoted by small letters (a, b, etc.). The 211 items encompass 255 bulae. The items are classified into six groups:

I: 1–10 — Bullae bearing titles of officials. This group, including one duplicate impression, numbers 11 bullae.

II: 11–168 — Bullae generally with two preserved names, that of the seal owner and that of his father (patronymic), or a least the name of the owner. This group represents 158 seals and, including duplicates, numbers 200 bullae.

III: 169–180 — Fragmentary bullae preserving only the patronymic of the seal-owner. None of these sealings are represented in the above groups, and only one duplicate bullae occurs.

IV: 181–198 — Fragmentary bullae preserving only parts of the name, which cannot confidently be restored. Some of these fragments may originally have been parts of identical bullae.

V: 199–206 — Bullae bearing ornamental motifs, with only portions of names preserved, or containing no characters whatsoever. Only two bullae (Nos. 204 and 205) were definitely anepigraphic. It is certain that the bullae of this group were not related to any of the bullae of the previous groups.

VI: 207–211 — Entirely illegible bullae.

The duplicate seals are as follows:

Nos. 1–2 (3 bullae)	Nos. 53–54 (2 bullae)
Nos. 17–18 (4 bullae)	Nos. 71–73 (3 bullae)
Nos. 20–21 (2 bullae)	Nos. 96–97 (2 bullae)
Nos. 22–23 (2 bullae)	Nos. 101–102 (2 bullae)
Nos. 24–26 (7 bullae)	Nos. 114–116 (4 bullae)
Nos. 39–40 (2 bullae)	Nos. 143–148 (9 bullae)
Nos. 43–46 (5 bullae)	Nos. 158–160 (3 bullae)

Thus, eight persons owned 2 seals each, four owned 3 seals each, one owned 4 seals and one owned 6 seals; that is, 38 seals were owned by only fourteen individuals.

From the above lists it emerges that the first two groups, I and II, present most of the data contained in the entire assemblage. Together they encompass 211 bullae impressed by 168 different seals, and all the names of their owners have been preserved. Including 43 duplicate impressions, these two groups contain 211 of the 255 bullae.

Groups III and IV provide fragmentary data. It is not always certain that particular fragments do not belong to identical bullae, or that particular fragmentary bullae do not belong to duplicate seals. In any event, we have sought to clarify this as far as possible and we are confident as to the result; certainly, any corrections would have little effect on a revised numbering of the bullae. Group V is a homogeneous group displaying few connections to the other groups, while group VI contributes little to our knowledge apart from its mere existence.

Thus, the entire assemblage of bullae numbers 255 items and, in light of the above, it would be reasonable to assume that at least 211 seals were originally employed to impress them.

2. THE BULLAE

A. Bullae with Official Titles

1–2. ʾAdoniyahu who is over the house

This official possessed two seals, of which three impressions have been found.

1

1. One bulla impressed with this seal measures 15×15.5 mm (size of impression: 12.5×15 mm). On the basis of the deep groove surrounding the impression, it can be assumed that the stone of this seal was set into a metal bezel (ring or pendant?). The bulla is divided into three horizontal registers by two double lines. The upper two registers contain the inscription, while the lower one is indistinct, giving the impression that there was some decorative motif there. The inscription reads:

(Belonging) to ʾAdoniyahu · לאדניהו
who is over the house אשר על הבית

2a

The script is fine and all the letters are clear, except for the blurred *aleph* in the second line. There is a division dot following the name at the end of the first line (for a discussion of this inscription, see below).

2. Two bullae, one complete (14.5 mm long) and the other damaged, were impressed with the second seal, which also seems to have been in a metal setting. The bulla is divided by a double line into two registers, surrounded by a double linear frame. The impression size is 10×12 mm. The text, as well as its division, are identical to those of the previous seal:

2b

(Belonging) to ʾAdoniyahu · לאדניהו
who is over the house אשר על הבית

Here, too, all the letters are clear, except for the second letter in the second line, which is blurred. Of all our assemblage, these two bullae provide the first examples of the calligraphic Hebrew script written in Judah during the 7th century BCE.

Both the seals used by ʾAdoniyahu, bearing the high-ranking title "who is over the house", were engraved by the same gem-cutter; this is clear from the absolutely identical script on both. As will be seen below, it was common for officials and other functionaries to use more than one seal in their affairs.

The owner of these seals, *ʾAdoniyahu*, cannot be identified. The Bible refers to three persons by this name: one of the sons of David, a Levite in the days of Jehoshaphat, and one of the leaders of the people in the days of Nehemiah. None of these three is suitable, chronologically, for our seal-owner lived at the end of the 7th century BCE. The name ʾAdoniyahu appears on three other bullae of our assemblage (Nos. 11, 125 and 165), as well as on Hebrew seals.[4] (For the title *ʾasher ʿal habbayit*, see below.)

3. Natan who is over the house

This bulla, fired black, is broken on the lower right. It is 16 mm long and has a two-line inscription divided by a double line:

(Belonging) to Natan who is	**לנתן אשר**
over (the) house	**[ע]ל בית**

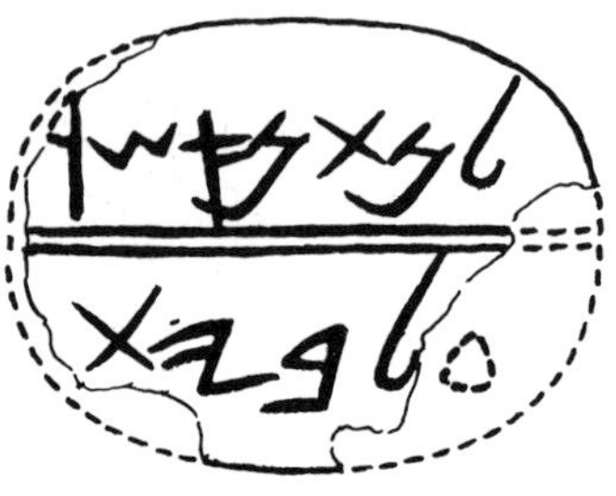

3

In the second line, the first letter is missing and should be restored as an *ʿayin*. The second word of the second line lacks the article *he*, probably an error.

The owner of this seal cannot be identified amongst the personages of the Bible. The bearers of this name include one of the sons of David, as well as the Prophet Nathan and the father of two of Solomon's ministers (1 Kings 4: 5). Zechariah 12: 12 mentions the "house of Nathan" as an important family early in the period of the monarchy.

The title *ʾasher ʿal habbayit*, "who is over (in charge of) the house", held by both ʾAdoniyahu and Natan, is interpreted as belonging to the official responsible for the

4 In the cases of names appearing in the Bible and on seals, and requiring no further discussion, we have not always cited bibliography. The reader is referred to Noth and to the tripartite bibliography published in Vattioni 1969, 1971 and 1978.

royal palace, the majordomo or palace prefect.[5] Holders of this title in the Bible were at the top of the hierarchy of the royal bureaucracy, though they did not always have the same degree of power. Ahishar *ʾasher ʿal habbayit* was one of Solomon's ministers (1 Kings 4: 6); Arza *ʾasher ʿal habbayit* served Elah, king of the northern Kingdom of Israel at Tirzah (1 Kings 16: 9); and Obadiah *ʾasher ʿal habbayit* was in charge of Ahab's palace at Samaria (1 Kings 18: 3). Jotham the son of Uzziah was in charge (*ʿal habbayit*) and ruled over the people during the days of his father's illness (2 Kings 15: 5).

Shebna, *ʾasher ʿal habbayit* in the days of Hezekiah, had great influence in state affairs and was the first among the royal ministers until he was reduced to the rank of scribe (Isaiah 22: 15ff.). He was replaced by Eliakim the son of Hilkiah at a festive, symbolic ceremony (2 Kings 18: 18; Isaiah 22: 20–24; 36: 3). Subsequent to Eliakim, no individual holding this title is mentioned in the Bible. In extra-biblical sources, the title is mentioned in a burial inscription ascribed conjecturally to the above-mentioned Shebna.[6] It also appears on the bulla of Gedalyahu *ʾasher ʿal habbayit* found at Lachish,[7] and on the seal of ʿIddo *ʾasher ʿal habbayit*, published recently.[8]

From the above discussion, it can be concluded that ʾAdoniyahu and Natan, represented by bullae Nos. 1–3, were high office-holders at the royal court. As contemporaries of Baruch the scribe, they may have served kings from Josiah up to Zedekiah. The Bible does not mention any official bearing this title during this period; but we also know of the seal-impression of Gedalyahu *ʾasher ʿal habbayit*, which is generally ascribed to the days of Zedekiah.

4

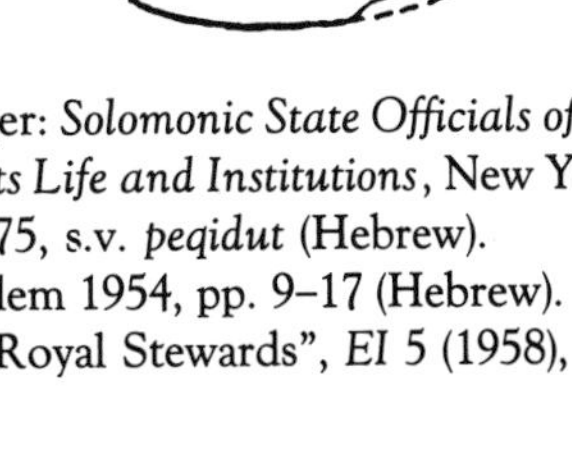

4. ʾElishamaʿ servant of the king

This bulla has been chipped away around the edges, but the inscription is preserved almost in its entirety. It has a two-line inscription divided by three parallel lines:

(Belonging) to ʾElishamaʿ	לאלשמע
servant of the king	[ע]בד המלך

The *ʿayin* at the end of the first line is slightly damaged, and that at the beginning of the second line is missing. The *ʾlšmʿ*, written here and on

5 For discussions of the officials involved, see T. N. D. Mettinger: *Solomonic State Officials of the Israelite Monarchy*, Lund 1971; R. de Vaux: *Ancient Israel, Its Life and Institutions*, New York 1961, pp. 119–142; S. Yeivin, in *Enṣ. Miqr*. VI, cols. 539–575, s.v. *peqidut* (Hebrew).

6 N. Avigad: *Ancient Monuments in the Kidron Valley*, Jerusalem 1954, pp. 9–17 (Hebrew). See also H. J. Katzenstein: "The House of Eliakim, a Family of Royal Stewards", *EI* 5 (1958), pp. 108–110 (Hebrew; English summary on pp. 89*–90*).

7 Moscati, p. 61: 30.

8 Avigad 1979, No. 9.

three other bullae in defective spelling, is vocalized ʾElishamaʿ in the MT. In the Bible, several persons of rank bearing this name are mentioned, but only one of them was among the royal ministers — Elishama the scribe, who served under Jehoiakim, king of Judah (Jeremiah 26: 12). Although Elishama the scribe was a contemporary of our seal-owner, ʾElishamaʿ servant of the king, the two should not be identified with one another, because of the difference in title. Though Elishama the scribe could have used the more general title "servant of the king", it is unlikely that the royal scribe would put aside his own title for another, less specific one which did not reflect his function. Nor should our ʾElishamaʿ be identified with "ʾElishamaʿ son of the king", appearing on a Hebrew seal, for the latter, according to his title, was of the royal family.

The title "servant of the king" is known as that of high officials at the court. Though in the Bible only one person is denoted specifically as such, Asaiah servant of the king (2 Kings 22: 12; 2 Chronicles 34: 20), we know that it was much more common, as is indicated by the numerous seals of persons bearing this title: Yaʾazanyahu servant of the king,[9] ʿObadyahu servant of the king,[10] Shemaʿ servant of the king,[11] and others. Furthermore, several seals have been found of other "servants", specifically of kings: Shemaʿ servant of (King) Yerobʿam,[12] ʾAshnaʾ servant of (King) ʾAḥaz,[13] Shebanyaw servant of (King) ʿUzziyaw,[14] and others. This title was apparently a rather general one and was not indicative of the type of office held, beyond the fact that its holder was a high-ranking official of the circle close to the king.

5. Gedalyahu servant of the king

This small, broken bulla lacks its left edge (its extant length is 10 mm). It has a double linear frame enclosing a two-line inscription divided by a double line:

(Belonging) to Gedalyahu לגדליהו
servant of the king עבד המלך

Enlarged 4:1

5

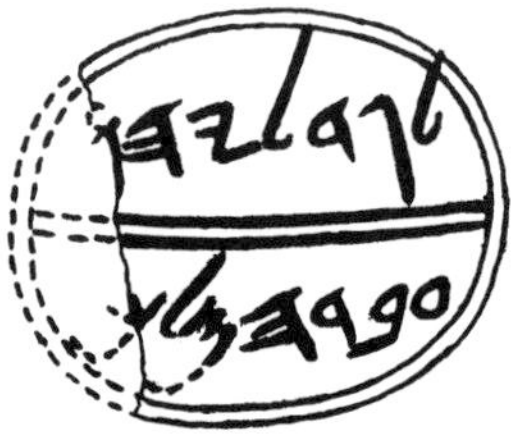

9 Diringer, No. 69.
10 Diringer, No. 70.
11 Diringer, No. 71.
12 Diringer, No. 68.
13 Moscati, p. 59: 21.
14 Diringer, No. 67.

The tiny script is fine. Only the final letter in the second line is truly damaged.

The name *Gedalyahu* is quite common, and the Bible notes two persons of this name in the days of Jeremiah, each of whom could have held the title "servant of the king". Gedaliah the son of Pashhur was one of Zedekiah's ministers who urged the king to put Jeremiah to death to prevent him from subverting the people during the Babylonian siege (Jeremiah 38: 61); he does not bear a specific title, as is the case with many ministers in the Bible. His seal, however, may have included the title which, as we have noted, was a rather general one for high officials. The other Gedalyahu was the son of Ahikam, a scion of a noble family which held various important offices in the Kingdom of Judah. His father, Ahikam the son of Shaphan, saved Jeremiah from death (Jeremiah 26: 24). His grandfather, Shaphan, was the scribe of King Josiah. After the destruction of Jerusalem, the Babylonians placed Gedaliah son of Ahikam in charge of those remaining behind in Judah (2 Kings 25: 22; Jeremiah 40: 5). It is assumed that the King of Babylon chose him for this task because he was of the nobility and had held high office under Zedekiah.

Many scholars identify Gedaliah son of Ahikam with the Gedalyahu *ʾasher ʿal habbayit* whose seal-impression was found at Lachish. The script of that bulla is absolutely identical with that of Gedalyahu servant of the king, with which we are dealing here. It is possible that these two officials were one and the same person, and that one of the bullae was impressed while he was still servant of the king and the other after he had attained the higher rank of "who is over the house". All these attempts at identification are, of course, entirely hypothetical.

6. Geʾalyahu son of the king

This complete and rather large bulla is fired black and measures 16×19 mm. On the basis of the deep groove around the impression, it would seem that the seal was in a metal setting. The bulla is divided into three registers, the upper one containing a stylized palmette rendered in the Phoenician manner, a form quite common on Hebrew seals[15] and on ivories.[16] Flanking the palmette there are two single dots. The inscription occupies the two lower registers:

(Belonging) to Geʾalyahu	**לגאליהו ב**
son of the king	**ן̇ המלך**

The script in the first line is somewhat blurred, due to the wearing of the seal-stone, but all the letters can be discerned. The *nun* at the beginning of the lower line is partly missing. Some of the fibres of the string have been preserved in the imprint of the string on the back of the bulla.

The name *Geʾalyahu* is not found in the Bible, but the name Igal (derived from the same Hebrew root, *gʾl*) is mentioned. However, the name does appear in the Arad inscriptions (39: 5; 16: 5). At the Beth-Zur excavations, a clay bulla was found

15 Diringer, Pl. 19: 25; Bordreuil-Lemaire 1982, Pl. 5: 2.
16 J. W. Crowfoot & G. M. Crowfoot: *Early Ivories from Samaria*, London 1938, Fig. 10, Pl. 21: 2.

reverse obverse 6

bearing an identical inscription "(Belonging) to Ge᾿alyahu son of the king".[17] The two bullae were impressed with different seals, for that from Beth-Zur bears no ornamental motif. Thus, this official also had two seals. Recently, a seal of another official of this name, but with a different title, was published: "Ge᾿alyahu servant of the king".[18] (For the title "son of the king", see below, bulla No. 8.)

7. Neriyahu son of the king

7

This bulla is broken above, and bears two lines of script divided by a double line:

(Belonging) to Neriyahu	לנרי[הו ב]
son of the king	ן המלך

In the first line, the *lamed*, *nun*, *resh* and a somewhat blurred *yod* are preserved, but the name can certainly be restored as *Neriyahu*. In the second line, the word *hammelekh* is clear, with traces of a *nun* before it. Thus, the restoration is quite certain. An unpublished seal bears the identical inscription "(Belonging) to Neriyahu son of the king" in its entirety,[19] but it differs from the present impression in that it bears an ornamental motif. Both seals apparently belonged to the same person. (For the title "son of the king", see below.)

17 Diringer, p. 127, No. 10.
18 W. J. Fulco: "A Seal from Umm el Qanafid, Jordan", *Orientalia* NS 48 (1979), p. 107.
19 To be published shortly in the forthcoming *F. M. Cross Festschrift*.

8. Yeraḥme᾽el son of the king[20]

Enlarged 4:1

8

This complete bulla is relatively small, measuring 10×12 mm. The linear frame measures 7×9 mm; it juts inward somewhat on the upper left, as a result of pressure on the soft clay after impression. There are two lines of script separated by a double line:

(Belonging) to Yeraḥme᾽el **לירחמאל**
son of the king **בן המלך**

The name Yeraḥme᾽el (Jerahmeel) appears in the Bible as the appellation of a tribal-ethnic unit, as well as the personal name of several individuals, including Jerahmeel the king's son, who was ordered, together with two other officials, to arrest Jeremiah and Baruch the scribe (Jeremiah 36: 26). Since our assemblage also includes a bulla of Baruch (see No. 9), it appears that we may identify with certainty the owner of this bulla with this same Jerahmeel the king's son.

The significance of the title "son of the king" is a matter of scholarly controversy. Some interpret it literally, claiming that the seal-owner was a member of the royal family, holding some function in the royal service.[21] In contrast, others hold that this was the title of a royal official unrelated to the king.[22]

The second interpretation is based on the fact that in the Bible five persons are described as "son of the king", and only one of these is known to have been of the royal family — Jotham son of Uzziah. Three others carried out functions connected with police and prison activities: Joash the king's son and Jerahmeel the king's son, who were involved in the arrest and imprisonment of the prophets Micaiah and Jeremiah, and of Baruch the scribe; and Maaseiah the king's son, mentioned in association with other officials.

Another important source concerning the use of this title is the seals. Four seals and five seal-impressions bearing this title are known: "᾽Elishamaᶜ son of the king", "Menashe son of the king", "Yeho᾽aḥaz son of the king", and "Neriyahu son of the king"— all on seals; and "Shebanyahu son of the king", "Ge᾽alyahu son of the king" (twice), "Yeraḥme᾽el son of the king", and "Neriyahu son of the king" — all on impressions. In this list, there are two names, Menashe and Yehoaḥaz, which are

20 First published in Avigad 1978a.

21 A. F. Rainey: "The Prince and the Pauper", *Ugarit-Forschungen* 7 (1975), pp. 427–432; A. Lemaire: "Note sur le titre BN HMLK dans l'ancien Israel", *Semitica* 29 (1979), pp. 59–65; and see recently Avigad 1981a.

22 G. Brin: "The Title בן (ה)מלך and its Parallels", *Annali dell'Istituto Orientale Universitario di Napoli* 29 (=NS 19) (1969), pp. 433–456; S. Yeivin, in *Enṣ. Miqr.* II, col. 160, s.v. *ben-hammelekh* (Hebrew).

known to have belonged to princes and kings. Despite this, doubts have been raised concerning the identification of the owners of these seals. The present author subscribes to the theory which assigns the persons bearing this title to the royal family; they were apparently of royal blood though not necessarily actual king's sons, and fulfilled various functions, including those connected with security of the kingdom. There were of course many scions of the royal family; they were often given some form of official occupation and in such capacities, these persons used seals during the performance of their duties.

From our bullae it is evident that Jerahmeel the king's son, who according to the Bible served in a police role, also dealt with matters involving the sealing of documents. Ge᾿alyahu son of the king (see No. 6) sealed documents using two different seals, impressions of which have been found at two different sites. This is surely indicative of the wide range of his activities.

9. Berekhyahu son of Neriyahu the scribe[23]

This complete bulla, of dark brown clay, measures 16×17 mm. The seal was oval (measuring 11×13 mm). It has a linear frame; the area within is divided by two double lines into three registers containing a three-line inscription:

(Belonging) to Berekhyahu	לברכיהו
son of Neriyahu	בן נריהו
the scribe	הספר

reverse

obverse

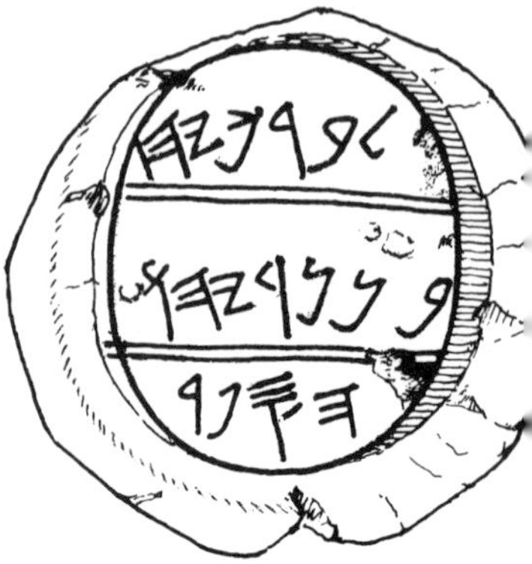

9

The inscription is complete; though the script is clear and well executed, it is not of the same high calligraphic standard as the previous bullae. The first line is well spaced at first, but toward the end the letters are crowded and no room was left for the head of the *waw*. In the second line there are quite large spaces between the letters of the first word, possibly caused by a flaw in the seal-stone. This is an

23 For the initial publication, see above, n. 20.

aesthetic flaw on the seal of a scribe, but its owner was apparently willing to overlook such a trivial matter.

The name *Berekhyahu* is quite common in the Bible. The word *hspr*, "the scribe", appears here in defective spelling, without the vowel *waw*, and it is rendered in this form on all the seals on which it occurs.

Scribes fulfilled an important role in the royal administration in Judah, as elsewhere in the ancient world.[24] Of particular importance was the royal scribe, who served as the king's personal secretary as well as secretary of state. Royal scribes such as Shebna the scribe, in the days of Hezekiah, and Shaphan the scribe under Josiah, played an especially important role in the official hierarchy. In the days of Jehoiakim, this office was held by Elishama the scribe (Jeremiah 36: 12). Gemariah son of Shaphan the scribe, who was a minister in that period, was apparently not a scribe himself but rather the son of a scribe, Shaphan.[25]

To date, only one Hebrew seal of a scribe has been published — that of "Mʾš son of Manoah the scribe"[26] (a second seal of this class, as yet inpublished, is in the Israel Museum). From the Persian period there is a Judahite bulla of "Yirmi the scribe", written in Aramaic script but in the Hebrew language (*hspr*).[27] Neither of these persons is mentioned in the Bible. Two Moabite seals are known bearing this title: "ʿAmoṣ the scribe" and "Kemoshʿam (son of) Kemoshʾel the scribe".[28] A Moabite bulla of this class is to be published shortly.

Baruch the son of Neriah the son of Mahseiah the scribe, who was of a noble Judean family, held a unique position among these scribes. This is the person who can be identified as the owner of the seal which impressed our bulla. The full form of his name was apparently Berekhyahu (Berechiah), a fact not previously known, for the Bible gives only the hypocoristic form Baruch (henceforth, we shall refer to him by this shorter form, for convenience). In the Hebrew Bible, his father's name is given in two forms, Neriyah and Neriyahu.

Baruch the scribe appears in the Bible as the personal secretary, friend and confidant of the Prophet Jeremiah. It was he who wrote down Jeremiah's prophecies in a scroll. When Baruch read out before the people Jeremiah's predictions of the destruction of Jerusalem, King Jehoiakim ordered Jerahmeel the king's son (see above, bulla No. 7) to seize him (Jeremiah 36: 26). This took place in Jehoiakim's fourth year, that is, in 605/604 BCE. This date provides a solid chronological base for the entire assemblage of bullae, and thus they can be ascribed quite definitely to the end of the 7th century and the beginning of the 6th century BCE. This matter will be discussed more fully in the concluding chapter.

24 See above, n. 5; cf. also B. Mazar: *Canaan and Israel, Historical Essays*, Jerusalem 1974, pp. 208–221 (Hebrew).
25 See below, n. 164.
26 P. Bordreuil, *Syria* 52 (1975), pp. 107–118.
27 Avigad 1976a, p. 7, No. 6.
28 See Hestrin-Dayagi, Nos. 1–2.

10. Governor of the city[29]

This bulla is slightly broken at the top; presently it measures 16×18 mm. The impression size is 11×13 mm. The clay is fired black. A deep groove surrounding the impression indicates that the seal-stone had been set into a metal bezel.

Within an oval linear frame is a depiction unique in the iconography of the Hebrew seals: two male figures, in pseudo-Assyrian style, stand opposite one another, both bearded, with long hair and dressed in long garments bearing a network pattern. The figure on the left is the larger of the two and holds in his outstretched left hand a bow and three arrows. The ends of the bow are curved outward like the head of a duck. His right hand rests on the hilt of a sword, shown jutting out behind his back. The lower end of a quiver (?) can be seen in the front, just below the waist.

The slightly smaller figure, on the right, is at a somewhat higher level. His left hand hangs straight down, while his right hand is raised toward the other figure in blessing. He wears no sword. Beneath the feet is a cartouche-like frame containing the inscription. The engraver of the seal apparently considered the iconographic aspect more important than the script, which is so small that it is difficult to read without magnification. Despite this, the script is very clear and the cartouche, a rare feature on Hebrew seals, serves to emphasize it.

The iconography of this bulla is influenced by Assyrian art. In Assyrian reliefs and on cylinder-seals, the motif of a king holding a bow and arrows (denoting power and rule), with one of his officials standing before him in a gesture of submission, is common.[30] However, the manner in which the smaller figure here holds out his hand, open toward the figure opposite, is Egyptian and can be seen in Phoenician art and elsewhere in the Near East. In Mesopotamian art the hand is held differently: open upward, or closed with one finger stretched out as a sign of blessing or prayer. The position of the hand and the schematic linear style of the figures point to the local workmanship of this seal.

The inscription within the cartouche is in a single line:

Governor of the city שר הער

The script is very small (the entire inscription is 4 mm long), but very carefully executed. The defective spelling of the second word lacks the vowel *yod*; this may be compared to similar spellings of such words as *ʾš* for *ʾyš*, "man", and *ym* for *ywm*, "day", in the Siloam Tunnel inscription. In contrast, note the full spelling of the same word, *ʿyr*, "city", in the Lachish Letters (4: 7) and in an Arad Inscription (24: 17).

29 For the initial publication, see Avigad 1976b, pp. 178–182.

30 See J. Pritchard: *The Ancient Near East in Pictures*, Princeton 1969, Figs. 351 (top) and 371. The king generally holds a bow in one hand and arrows in the other, but sometimes they are both held in one hand. See R. D. Barnett: *Assyrian Palace Reliefs*, London 1960, Pl. 97; idem, *Sculptures from the North Palace of Ashurbanipal at Nineveh (668–631 B.C.)*, London 1975, Pl. 59 (bottom).

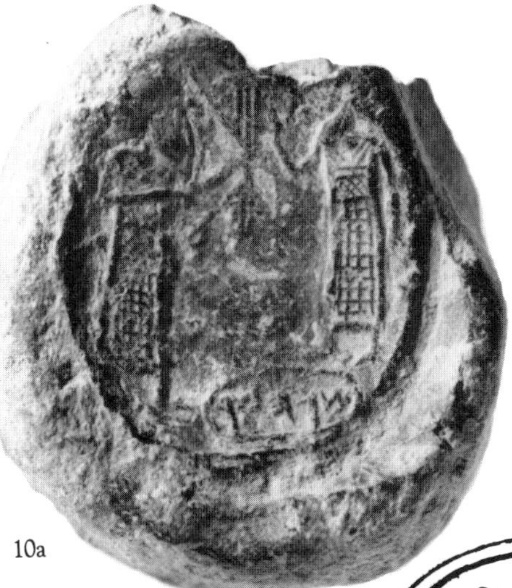

10a

10b

Enlarged 4:1

Duplicate impression not found together with the other bullae (see page 32)

This brief inscription, which omits the possessive *lamed* and lacks a personal name, comprises only the title of its owner, in sharp contrast to the personal seals of officials, which invariably bear the name of their owners. Thus, we have before us a unique anonymous, official seal bearing only the titulary, which could have served successive office-holders bearing the title "governor of the city". The anonymous character of the seal leads us to assume that a city governor received the seal upon assumption of his office, and that it was not made especially for him; if this had been the case, it would surely have borne his personal name.

The title *śar haʿir*, "governor of the city" is otherwise unknown on seals but occurs in the Bible. It is held by senior officials appointed by the king who were responsible for a city. Several such title-bearers are noted in the Bible by name: we find "Zebul the ruler of the ciry" in the period of the Judges, (Judges 9: 30); "Amon the governor of the city" of Samaria (who imprisoned Micaiah the Prophet upon the order of King Ahab; 1 Kings 22: 26); "Maaseiah the governor of the city (who was ordered to repair the Temple by Josiah: 2 Chronicles 34: 8); and "Joshua the governor of the city" (after whom was named a city gate, apparently in Jerusalem:

2 Kings 23: 8). One of the ministers of Samaria in the days of Jehu was entitled *ʾasher ʿal hair*, "who is over the city" (together with a minister whose title was *ʾasher ʿal habbayit*); however, his name is not mentioned (2 Kings 10: 5). It would seem that only capital cities were governed by officials bearing this title, and thus it is likely that our bulla was sealed by the governor of Jerusalem. One biblical passage has led some scholars to conclude that Jerusalem had more than one governor: "Then Hezekiah the king rose early and gathered the *śarei ha ʿir* and went up to the house of the Lord" (2 Chronicles 29: 20). But the intention there seems to be not all those holding this title, but all the *śarim* residing in the city.

As noted above, the seal with which our bulla was impressed is the first Hebrew seal bearing this Assyrian motif. It is surprising that of all the officials' seals known to us, it is the seal of the governor of the city which bears a scene demonstrating the royal authority — a most unexpected motif on an official seal in the Kingdom of Judah.

The iconography of the Hebrew seals generally employs Egyptian motifs common in Phoenician art. The use of an obviously Assyrian theme, such as that before us, on the seal of a city governor may point to a period of Assyrian influence in Jerusalem. The reign of Manasseh, who was a loyal vassal of Assyria (698–642 BCE), would be such a period, but it must be borne in mind that our assemblage contains sealings from the end of the 7th century BCE. However, if it is presumed that the archive to which these bullae belonged preserved documents over a period of several decades, we might ascribe the seal of the city governor to the mid-7th century BCE and assume that it was used by a series of officials, as suggested above.

The inscription is, of course, of special interest. The title appears here for the first time on a seal, and is thus a significant addition to the limited number of titles known from seals.[31] Indeed, this bulla is the first vivid evidence of the administrative activities of an official responsible for a city administration in the days of the Judean monarchy. The city was surely the capital and not an outlying, secondary town, and the anonymous official was certainly the mayor of Jerusalem.[32]

*

After the preliminary publication of this bulla, G. Barkay published an identical bulla.[33] No information as to its provenance was given, but to the best of my

31 At Kuntillet ʿAjrud on the western border of the Negev, pottery jars were found bearing personal names incised in Hebrew, such as *ʿyrʾ* and *ʿdh*. Four jars bear the word *lśrʿr*; Z. Meshel: *Kuntillet ʿAjrud — A Religious Centre from the Time of the Judaean Monarchy on the Border of Sinai* (Israel Museum Catalogue 175), Jerusalem 1978, p. 18. Following the discovery of the "governor of the city" bullae, it was suggested that the Kuntillet ʿAjrud inscription should also be interpreted as *le-śar ha-ʿir*, in a defective spelling and without the article *he-*, and that it be regarded as the title of the official governing that place. Since the site is known to have been a single structure (or two buildings at most), which served as a way-station on the desert highway, it is highly doubtful that the local commander would have held so lofty a rank. *Śrʿr* may in fact be an unknown personal name, like those incised on the other storage-jars.

32 For the title "governor of the city", see de Vaux, *op. cit.* (above, n. 5), pp. 137–138.

33 G. Barkay: "A Second Bulla of the 'Governor of the City'", *Qadmoniot* 10 (1977/78), pp. 69–71 (Hebrew).

knowledge it cannot be associated with the present assemblage of bullae, for it was purchased from a Jerusalem antiquities dealer several years before the discovery of our bullae. A photograph of this bulla (No. 10b) was obtained by the present author around the time of its purchase (by A. Kindler, Director of the Kadman Numismatic Museum of the Haaretz Museum in Tel Aviv). The two bullae were impressed from the very same seal. This duplicate bulla is the clearer of the two in several aspects, such as the faces of the figures and the form of the bow. Barkay has interpreted the scene as a depiction of the installation of the seal owner as governor of the city, as it actually took place. He writes, *inter alia*: "Before us, apparently, is a depiction of a particular ceremony connected with the owner of the seal, and it is logical to assume that this was the ceremony in which the king invested his authority in the governor of the city. The hand of the governor of the city is stretched out to receive the bow and arrows from the king". This interpretation, though very interesting, is entirely unconvincing.[34] The scene is a standardized theme deriving from the Assyrian reliefs, where the king holds a bow and arrows as symbols of his rule, while the other figure, a loyal official, raises his hand in submission, not to receive the weapons. Throughout the abundant art of Mesopotamia, we have found no graphic expression of such a ceremony, in which a king grants symbols of his authority to a subordinate. Moreover, if the owner of the seal had intended to commemorate such a ceremony on his seal, he would certainly have perpetuated his name as well.

B. Bullae with the Name and Patronymic of the Owner

11. ʾAdoniyahu son of Yeqamyahu

Two fragments join to form a complete bulla (the two parts are in the two different collections). It is 14 mm long and contains two lines of script with a double line between them:

11

(Belonging) to ʾAdoniyahu	לארניהו ב
son of Yeqamyahu	ן יקמיהו

The script is fine. The word *ben* is divided between the two lines, as is common on seals. The name *ʾAdoniyahu* is discussed above, under bulla No. 1. The name *Yeqamyahu* is found on several bullae (see below), on seals and in the Arad inscriptions (1: 39; 2: 59). The Bible mentions Jekamiah son of Shallum among the descendants of Jerahmeel (1 Chronicles 2: 41), and Jekamiah the son of Jehoiakim, king of Judah (1 Chronicles 3: 18).

34 See my response in *Qadmoniot* 11 (1977/78), p. 34 (Hebrew).

12

13

14

12. Pedayahu (son of) Yehoqam

This bulla is damaged on the upper edge; it is 15 mm long. The linear frame is 10 mm long and contains a two-line inscription divided by a double line:

(Belonging) to Pedayahu לפדיהו
(son of) Yehoqam יהוקם

The letters are large and widely spaced, and some are blurred. The reading of the first name, *Pedayahu*, is uncertain. The second name, *Yehoqam*, is not found in the Bible; it is the Qal form, in the past tense, of the well-known names Yeqamyahu and Yehoyaqim. It appears on Hebrew seals.

13. ʾAḥiyahu (son of) ʾAbiyahu

This bulla is broken on three edges; a linear frame encloses a two-line inscription divided by a double line:

(Belonging) to ʾAḥiyahu [לא]חיהו
(son of) ʾAbiyahu [א]ביהו

The first letters of both lines are missing. *ʾAbiyahu* (Abijah) occurs in the Bible as the name of a king of Judah (2 Chronicles 13: 20). On seals this name is found only in the shorter form *ʾabyw*. For the name *ʾAḥiyahu*, see bulla No. 166.

14. ʾAḥiqam son of Ṭobiyahu

This bulla is divided into three registers by double lines. The upper register contains a Phoenician palmette motif (see bulla No. 6), common on Hebrew seals[35] and on ivories.[36] The inscription is in the two lower registers:

(Belonging) to ʾAḥiqam son of לאחקם ב[ן]
Ṭobiyahu טביהו

The script is careless and slightly blurred. The name *ʾAḥiqam* is also found on the two following bulla. The Bible mentions Ahikam son of Sha-

35 Diringer, Pl. 19: 25.
36 See above, n. 16.

phan, one of the more important ministers in the days of Josiah (2 Kings 22: 12). This name is found in the full spelling on seals: *ʾḥyqm/mtn*,[37] as well as in the Arad Ostraca (5: 31): *ʾḥyqm bn šm ʿyhw*. The name *ṭbyhw* appears with identical spelling in the Lachish Letters (19: 3). In 2 Chronicles 17: 8, it is vocalized טוֹבִיָּהוּ. Note also Tobiah the Ammonite servant (Nehemiah 2: 10).

15

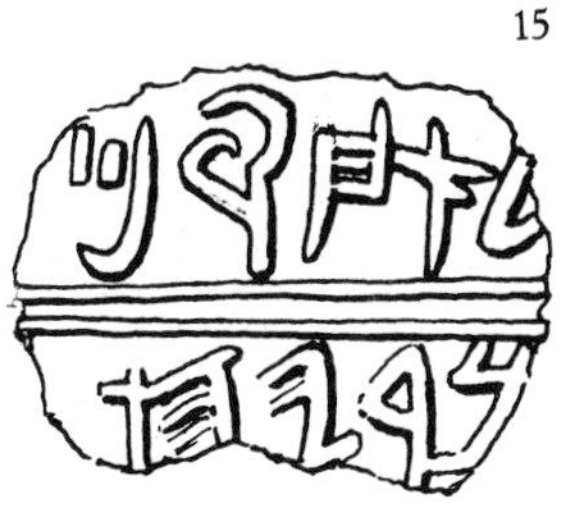

15. ʾAḥiqam (son of) Neriyahu

This bulla is damaged on the bottom edge. It has no margins. The two-line inscription is divided by two parallel lines:

(Belonging) to ʾAḥiqam לאחקם
(son of) Neriyahu נריהו

The script is upright, large and coarse. The peculiar *qoph* in the first name and the *ḥet* with a very tall foot are noteworthy. The name *ʾAḥiqam* is discussed above. The name *Neriyahu* is common in our assemblage. Some of the letters are somewhat damaged, but the reading is certain.

16. ʾAḥiqam (son of) ʾAḥʾab

This bulla is made up of two fragments. No margins appear in the impression. The two-line inscription is divided by a double line:

(Belonging to) ʾAḥiqam אחקם
(son of) ʾAḥʾab אחאב

The script is large and coarse. For the name *ʾAḥiqam*, see above; for the name *ʾAḥʾab*, see below.

16

17–18. ʾEl(i)ʿaz son of ʾAḥʾab

This person possessed two almost identical seals, differing only in the division of the inscription. Four bullae were impressed with these seals.

17. A complete bulla with linear frame and two lines dividing the two-line inscription. The upper

37 Avigad 1979, p. 127, No. 6.

17

line is well spaced, while the lower line is crowded because of the addition of the word *ben*:

(Belonging) to ʾEl(i)ʿaz	**לאלעז**
son of ʾAḥʾab	**בן אחאב**

The name *ʾlʿz* appearing on several bullae is found in the full spelling *ʾlyʿz* on two other bullae (see No. 28). It also appears on Ammonite seals.[38] The biblical names Eluzai and Uziel are related to it. For the name *ʾAhʾab*, see bulla No. 9.

18. Three impressions from this seal are included in the assemblage, two complete (a–b) and one broken (c). The two-line inscription is divided by a double line:

(Belonging) to ʾEl(i)ʿaz son of	**לאלעז בן**
ʾAḥʾab	**אחאב**

The script is large and careless. The division of the letters differs from No. 17; the script above is crowded, while that below is well spaced. The lower line is somewhat blurred.

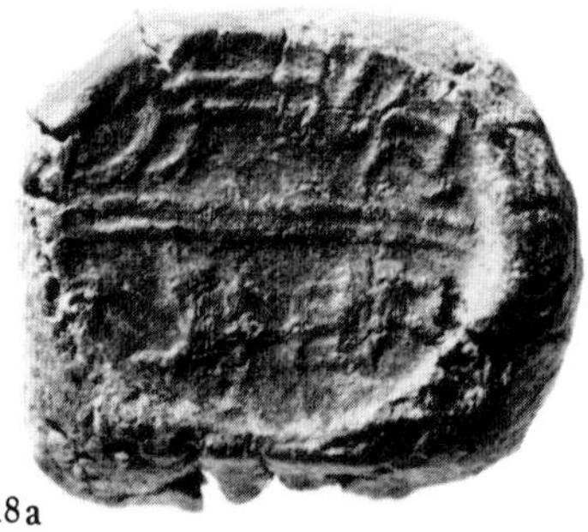

18a

18b

18c

38 Avigad 1954, p. 150; C. E. Puech: *Revue biblique* 83 (1976), pp. 59–62.

19. ʾAḥʾab son of ʾEphraḥ

19

This bulla is broken on the upper edge; it is 14 mm long and the impression is 9 mm long. A double linear frame encloses a two-line inscription divided by a double line. The upper line of script is somewhat damaged, but the reading is certain:

(Belonging) to ʾAḥʾab	**לאחאב**
son of ʾEphraḥ	**בן אפרח**

The script is fine. The name *ʾAḥʾab* is known in the Bible mainly as that of the king of Israel. It is also very frequent on seals and is found on two other bullae. The name *ʾEphraḥ*, which does not appear in the Bible, was apparently quite common, for it appears on two other bullae and on two seals: "ʾEphraḥ son of Semakyahu",[39] and "ʾEphraḥ son of ʾAḥʾab"[40] (note the identical names on our bulla, but in reverse order). The name ʾEphraḥ also appears among the bullae recently found in the City of David excavations.[41] Earlier, I interpreted the name as deriving from אֶפְרֹחַ, "chick". Though such an interpretation cannot entirely be ruled out, I would today prefer a derivation from the root *prḥ*, "blossoming, flourishing",[42] with the *aleph* as a prefix, and a reading of ʾEphraḥ. Compare the form of the biblical word *ʾephlal*, from the root *pll*, or *ʾpṣḥ* (in Samaria Ostracon 31), derived from *pṣḥ*; compare also the Akkadian *pirḫu*,[43] meaning "shoot, branch", which also serves as a personal name, and *prḫ* in Ugaritic.[44] Similarly, the biblical name Paruah (1 Kings 4: 17) also derives from *prḥ*.[45]

20–21. ʾEphraḥ son of Yehoshuaʿ

This person possessed two seals, on one of which his name and patronymic appear (as was usual), while on the other his grandfather's name was also given.

20. This bulla is somewhat damaged on the right edge. The two-line inscription is divided by a triple line. The two initial letters of the inscription are erased. At the end of the second line there is a branch motif serving as a space filler:

39 Avigad 1969, p. 7: 5.
40 Hestrin-Dayagi, No. 51 (the name ʾAḥʾab is not deciphered there).
41 Shiloh 1984.
42 M. Heltzer & M. Ohana: *The extra-Biblical Tradition of Hebrew Personal Names*, Haifa 1978, pp. 35, 138 (Hebrew).
43 Tallqvist, p. 181.
44 Gröndahl, pp. 312, 406.
45 *Enṣ. Miqr.* VI, col. 581 (Hebrew).

20

21

(Belonging) to ᵓEphraḥ son of Yehoshuaᶜ	**[לא]פרח בן יהושע**

The restoration of the name *ᵓEphraḥ* is certain. This name had been discussed in the previous entry. The name *Yehoshuaᶜ* (Joshua) is, of course, known from the Bible and is found on seals.

21. This bulla, 15 mm long and fired black, is divided into three registers by double lines. The inscription extends over all three registers. The script in the two upper registers is somewhat blurred, but the reading there is virtually certain:

(Belonging) to ᵓEphraḥ son of Yehoshuaᶜ son of Mattanyahu	**לאפרח ב ן יהושע בן מתניהו**

This is an impression from the second seal, giving the name of the grandfather, Mattanyahu. Mention of the third generation on a seal is rather unusual. Although among all the published Hebrew seals there are only two or three such instances, our assemblage of bullae contains five bullae of this type. It is generally assumed that the owner of such a seal was of a noble family. The name *Mattanyahu*, and its shorter form Mattanyah, are common in the Bible and on seals, and it appears on another bulla as well.

22–23. ᵓEphraḥ son of Shaḥar

This person also possessed two seals, one of which gives his patronymic and the other of which also gives the name of his grandfather. A single bulla of each seal is included in the assemblage.

22. Of this bulla only the left side has survived; it contains two lines of script divided by a triple line:

(Belonging) to ᵓEphraḥ son of Shaḥar	**[לא]פ̇רח [בן] שחר**

In each line only the final two and a half letters have survived, but the restoration

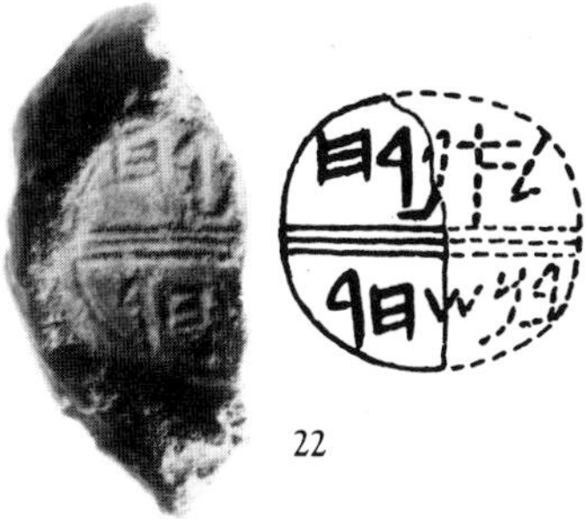

22

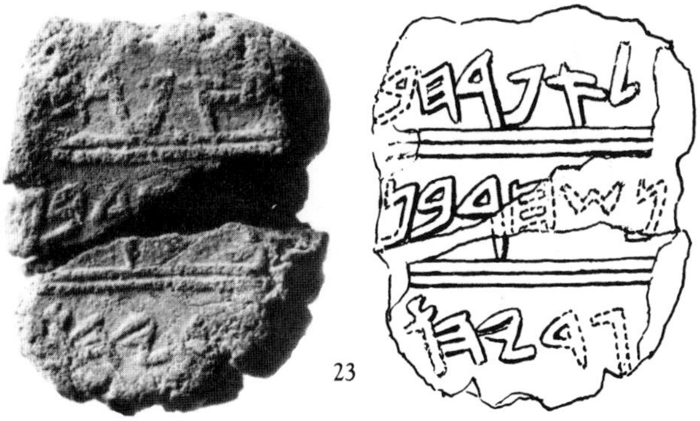

23

is certain. The name *ʾEphraḥ* has been treated above (bulla No. 19). For the name *Shaḥar*, see below, bulla No. 26.

23. This is a broken bulla pieced together from two fragments. The clay is fired black. It is 15 mm long and is divided into three registers by two double lines. The inscription occupies all three registers (there is a large gap in the middle register):

(Belonging) to ʾEphraḥ	**לאפרח [ב**
son of Shaḥar son of	**ן שח]ר בן**
Gaddiyahu	**[ג]ד̇יהו**

Only the first name is complete. Most of the patronymic is lacking, and the grandfather's name is damaged. In restoring the inscription, we were guided by the previous impression of ʾEphraḥ son of Shaḥar and by the following impressions of Shaḥar son of Gaddiyahu (bullae Nos. 24–26). For the names *Shaḥar* and *Gaddiyahu* see below. This is the second seal of the assemblage which includes three generations.

24–26. Shaḥar son of Gaddiyahu

This person possessed three different seals, of which seven bullae and bullae fragments were found:

24. Four bullae are impressed with this seal. On two bullae (a, b) the inscription is in its preserved entirety. The outer frame of the impression has not been preserved intact on any one bulla, but it can be reconstructed by combining the four bullae. The outer linear frame is of truncated lentoid form (16×8 mm), with a vertical strip at either end containing a running pattern of three pomegranates (see bulla No. 24a). This is an unusual arrangement among known seals. The two-line inscription is divided by a double line:

(Belonging) to Shaḥar son of	**לשחר בן**
Gaddiyahu	**גדיהו**

The small, elegant script is in classical Hebrew style. On bulla No. 24c, the upper

24 a

24b

24c

24d

25 a

26

25b

line is preserved in its entirety, but only three letters of the second line remain. On bulla No. 24d, the entire first line and the last three letters of the second line are preserved. For the names, see below.

25. The second seal is quite different from the above. Two bullae were impressed with this seal, one of which is almost complete, while of the second only a small fragment remains. Bulla No. 25a is joined from two fragments (each of which is in a different collection). The left edge is broken. The bulla is 10 mm wide. The outer frame consists of a ladder pattern. The two lines of script are divided by a triple line:

(Belonging) to Shaḥar	לשחר [ב]
son of Gaddi	ן גדי

The script here is not as fine as on the previous seal. In the first line only the last letter, *bet*, is missing. In the second line, the engraver did not space the letters carefully and no room was left for the ending of the full form of the name *Gaddiyahu*, resulting in the shortened form, Gaddi. Compare the name Gaddi the son of Susi, in Numbers 13: 11, and Gadi the father of King Menahem (2 Kings 15: 14).

26. Of this seal, the third of this group, there is only one bulla, which has been chipped, leaving a round shape. Four letters are preserved in the upper line of script, and three in the lower line. Two lines divide the two-line inscription. The letters are larger than those of the two previous seals:

(Belonging) to Shaḥar (son of)	**לשחר**
Gaddiyahu	**[ג]דיה[ו]**

Neither of these two names, Shaḥar or Gaddiyahu, is found in the Bible. *Shaḥar* is a hypocoristic form of the biblical names Shehariah and Ahishahar. It is common in our assemblage and found also on several seal-impressions on jars.[46] The name *Gaddiyahu* is parallel to the biblical name Gaddiel; it also appears on seals.[47] In the Samaria Ostraca it appears in the shorter form *gdyw*.

It may be noted that a certain Shaḥar was the father of ʾEphraḥ on bullae Nos. 22–23. Both these persons were quite active in the sealing of documents, and each of them had more than one seal.

27. ʾEliyahu son of Mikha

This bulla, partly damaged, is fired black. It bears a two-line inscription divided by a double line. The inscription is blurred but can be read:

(Belonging) to ʾEliyahu	**[ל]אליהו ב**
son of Mikha	**[ן] מיכה**

These two names appear in the Bible, both as names of prophets. The name *ʾlyhw* is vocalized in the Bible as אֵלִיָּהוּ (the prophet Elijah and several other persons) or as אֵלִיהוּ (a number of individuals). It is also found on seals and on pottery vessels. The name *Mikha* is a shortened form of Mikhayahu and also appears on the seal-impressions from the Persian period mentioned above.

27

46 Vattioni 1969, Nos. 198 and 199.
47 Moscati, p. 59: 22; Vattioni 1969, No. 142; P. Bordreuil & A. Lemaire: *Semitica* 29 (1979), p. 71: 1.

28

28. ʾEliʿaz son of Hoshaʿyahu

This bulla is damaged. It has a linear frame and a two-line inscription divided by two lines:

(Belonging) to ʾEliʿaz	**לאליעז**
son of Hoshaʿyahu	**בן הושעי[הו]**

The script is blurred but legible. The name *ʾEliʿaz* is spelled here with the *yod*, in contrast to the defective form appearing on bullae Nos. 17–18. The last two letters of the name *Hoshaʿyahu* are missing in the impression.

29

29. ʾEliram (son of) Shemaʿyahu

This bulla is broken on three sides. It bears a two-line inscription divided by two lines:

(Belonging) to ʾEliram	**לאלירם**
(son of) Shemaʿyahu	**שמעיהו**

The script is in high relief; the final letter in each line is blurred. The name *ʾEliram* is not mentioned in the Bible. However, it appears on several seals, in defective spelling: *ʾlrm/ḥsdyh* on a Hebrew seal[48] and *ʿbdʾ nʿr ʾlrm* on an Ammonite seal.[49] This is the first instance of a full spelling of this name with *yod*. The name *Shemaʿyahu* is very common among the bullae.

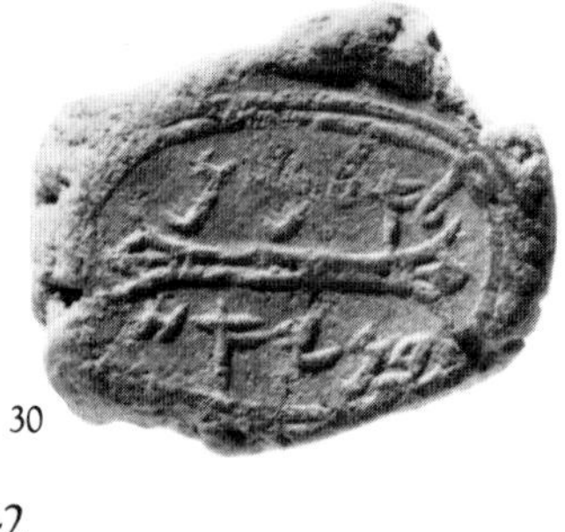

30

30. ʾElnatan son of Yaʾush

This bulla has a complete, oval impression, measuring 13×9 mm. The double linear frame encloses a two-line inscription divided by a double line terminating at either end in a lily design:

(Belonging) to ʾElnatan	**לאלנ[ת]ן**
son of Yaʾush	**בן יאש**

The script is fine. In the upper line, the fifth letter is erased, but should probably be restored as a *taw*. The fourth letter could be a *mem*, but a *nun* is preferable.

48 Vattioni 1969, No. 220.
49 Avigad 1964, p. 192.

The name ʾ*Elnatan* in the Bible belongs to several persons, including the father-in-law of Jehoiakim, king of Judah, and Elnathan the son of Achbor, one of Jehoiakim's generals. It is also found on seals and appears in one of the Lachish Letters (3: 15). The name *yʾš*, appearing on two other bullae, is probably related to the name *yʾwš*, in a full spelling, which occurs in the Lachish Letters (2: 1; 3: 2) and the Elephantine Papyri.[50] Yaʾush is a hypocoristic form of the biblical theophoric name *yʾšyhw* (Josiah), which appears once in Jeremiah 27: 1. These names are derived from the root *ʾwš*, which in South Arabian and Ugaritic means "to give". Accordingly, the meaning of the name Yaʾush would be "may He give".[51] Compare also the name *ʾšyhw*, "Yahweh has given", on bulla No. 33.

31. ʾAmaryahu son of Yehoʾab

Both bullae of this seal are broken on the right edge. The curved lines separating the first and third lines of the three-line inscription terminate on the surviving left in two papyrus flowers. The two letters of the middle line of script, forming the word *bn*, "son of", are placed between these terminating flowers (compare bulla No. 70). The inscription thus reads:

(Belonging) to ʾAmaryahu	**[ל]אמריהו**
son of	**ב ן**
Yehoʾab	**יהואב**

The script is tiny and fine. On bulla No. 31a, which is fired black, only the *lamed* at the beginning of the inscription is lacking. On bulla No. 31b, which is fired brown, the *lamed* and part of the *aleph* are missing. In the second line, the *bet* of the word *bn* is missing, and in the third line part of the *yod*.

The biblical name ʾ*Amaryahu* is common, and was typical of several priestly families who took part in the Return from Exile in the Persian period. It also appears on a Hebrew seal: *lyšʿyhw/ʾmryhw*; on an Ammonite seal there is the variant *ʾmrʾl*.[52] The name *Yehoʾab* is the first known instance of the full form of the biblical name Joab.

31a

31b

50 Cowley, Nos. 22: 89 and 39: 4.

51 *Enṣ. Miqr.* III, cols. 416–417, s.v. *Yoʾshiyahu* (Hebrew).

52 Avigad 1970, p. 286: 1.

32

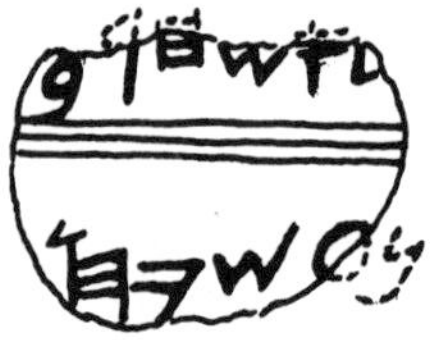

32. ʾAshḥur son of ʿAśayahu

This bulla is damaged at the top. The two-line inscription is divided by a double line:

(Belonging) to ʾAshḥur	לאשחר ב
son of ʿAśayahu	[ן] עשיהו

The script in the first line is partly damaged, but it is possible to distinguish most of the letters *ʾšḥr*, which seems to be the biblical name ʾAshḥur (Ashur), mentioned as the "father of Tekoa" (Chronicles 2: 24). The meaning of the name is disputed; some hold that it is a divine name from the Hurrian, Hittite or Egyptian pantheon (with the element *ḥwr*).[53] Thus, it would be a combination of the elements *ʾš*, derived from "to give", and *ḥwr*, yielding a meaning of "Ḥur gave"; the similar name ʾAshyahu is treated under the next item. The name *ʿAśayahu* is common in the Bible in the shorter form Asaiah. It is also found on other bullae and on seals. Compare, too, the name Maʿaśeyahu, below, bulla No. 87.

33

33. ʾAshyahu son of Shemaʿyahu

This bulla is slightly broken on the lower left, but the inscription is complete. It has a double linear frame enclosing a fine two-line inscription divided by two lines.

(Belonging) to ʾAshyahu	לאשיהו
son of Shemaʿyahu	בן שמעיהו

The name *ʾAshyahu* does not appear in the Bible but is found on two bullae of other persons (Nos. 105, 110). This name first appeared on the three seals of ʾAshyahu discovered at Arad (Nos. 105– 107) and on Arad Ostracon No. 51, which mentions ʾAshyahu son of ʿEzer. It has since been found on several other seals. The name ʾAshyahu is merely the inverted form of the biblical name Yehoash and is related to the names Yoshiyahu, Yoash and Yaʾush (see above, bulla No. 30), all ultimately derived from the root *ʾwš*, meaning "to give" in South Arabian and Ugaritic. In Ugaritic, *ušn* has the meaning of "gift". Accordingly, the meaning of ʾAshyahu would resemble that of Netanyahu ("Yahweh has given").[54] The biblical name *Shemaʿyahu* is common on our bullae.

53 *Enṣ. Miqr.* I, col. 760 (Hebrew).

54 E. Lipiński: "אשבעל and אשיהו and Parallel Personal Names", *Orientalia Lovaniensia Periodica* (1974), pp. 5–13.

34. ʾAsherḥai (son of) ʿAśayahu

34

This bulla is partly broken. It has a linear frame enclosing a two-line inscription divided by two lines which are not entirely parallel. At the end of the inscription there is a small branch serving as a space filler:

(Belonging) to ʾAsherḥai [לאש]רחי
(son of) ʿAśayahu עשיהו

The beginning of the upper line is severely damaged and only the three final letters (*rḥy*) are clear. The suggested reconstruction of the name is not certain, but is based on the few traces visible at the beginning of the line, which can be interpreted as an *aleph*; thus, the most likely name would be *ʾAsherḥai*, attested on bulla No. 126 (for the meaning of the name, see the entry for this bulla). The name *ʿAśayahu* (Asaiah) is common in the Bible and on seals.

Among the letters of the script here, we may note especially the square *ʿayin* and the *shin* of decidedly Aramaic form, with the middle stroke descending well below. The occurrence of such a *shin* among our bullae is an anomaly which is difficult to explain.

35. Benayahu (son of) ʿAliyahu

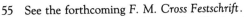

35

This is a complete bulla; the impression is 11 mm long. The outer linear frame encloses a two-line inscription divided by a double line:

(Belonging) to Benayahu לבניהו
(son of) ʿAliyahu עליהו

The name *Benayahu* is common in the Bible and on seals, and is also found in the Arad Ostraca (39: 9). The name *ʿAliyahu*, found on two other bullae, is previously unknown. It derives from the root *ʿly*, and means "Yahweh is high, exalted". Variants of this name are found on seals: *ʿlyw*,[55] *yhwʿly*[56] and *ywʿly*.[57] See also the biblical name *ʿly* (vocalized ʿEli), which is apparently a secondary, contracted form. To the same group belongs a seal reading: *ʿlh*.[58]

55 See the forthcoming F. M. Cross *Festschrift*.
56 Unpublished seal, as well as in the Elephantine Papyri, as a feminine name (Cowley, No. 22: 105).
57 A. Lemaire, *EI* 18 (1985), p. 29*, No. 1. The name is erroneously read there as *ywʿlyhw*.
58 A. Lemaire, *Semitica* 29 (1979), p. 67.

36

36. Baʿadiyahu (son of) . . .

This bulla is damaged. The two-line inscription is divided by a double line. The lower line of script is completely erased:

(Belonging) to Baʿadiyahu	**לבעדיהו**
. . . . .	. . . . .

The script is fine. The first name is well preserved. *Baʿadiyahu*, a new name on seals, is not mentioned in the Bible. It does appear, however, in the Elephantine Papyri, in the shorter form *bʿdyh*, omitting the final *waw*.[59] The name contains the preposition *bʿd*, "for", and is interpreted as "Yahweh is for me, protects me", in accordance with Psalms 3: 3 (MT vs. 4): "But thou, O Lord, art a shield about me (*magen baʿadi*)." A Hebrew seal from Beth-Shemesh bears the name *bʿdʾl*.[60] Compare a Phoenician seal recently published: *ʾlbʿdy*, "God is on my behalf", containing the preposition *bʿd* with the personal suffix *yod*.[61] See also the following bulla. The patronymic is lacking.

37

37. Baʿadiyahu (son of) Śerayahu

This bulla, which is partly damaged, is 15 mm long. The two-line inscription is divided by a design of two curved lines terminating in small circles and connected by short vertical lines at the centre and double triangles at either end:

(Belonging) to Baʿadiyahu	**לבעדיה[ו]**
(son of) Śerayahu	**שריהו**

The first name, *Baʿadiyahu*, is difficult to read in the photograph, but all the letters are present except for the *waw* which for lack of space, is barely distinguishable. Compare also the preceding bulla, and see the discussion there.

The name *Śerayahu* also occurs on bulla No. 167 and on seals. In the Bible it appears only once in this full form: Śeraiah (*Śryhw*) the son of Azriel, an

59 Cowley, Nos. 19: 2 and 25: 18.
60 Avigad 1953, p. 47 (Hebrew).
61 P. Bordreuil: *Atti del I Congresso Internationale di Studi Fenici e Punici* 3 (1983), pp. 753–754.

official of Jehoiakim mentioned together with Jerahmeel the king's son (Jeremiah 36: 26). In a shorter form (*Śryh*) it is frequent, for example Seraiah the son of Neriah, the brother of Baruch the scribe (Jeremiah 51: 59).[62] The first component of the name is interpreted as deriving from the root *śrh*, meaning "struggle, strive", as found in the ancient *Midrash* on the name 'Israel': "And in his manhood he strove (*śrh*) with God" (Hosea 12: 3 [MT vs. 4]), and "for you have striven (*śryt*) with God and with men, and have prevailed" (Genesis 32: 28 [MT vs. 29]). However, in the light of the name *śrmlk* on seals,[63] the name may be read Śaryahu, meaning "Yahweh is a prince (*śr*)". The Hebrew word *śar* is also a synonym for king, and hence Śariyahu and Malkiyahu might be parallel in meaning.

38. Berekhyahu son of Shemaʿyahu

This bulla is composed of two fragments in the two different collections. The right part is missing. The two-line inscription is divided by a "bud design" with a circle at the middle — a common motif on Hebrew seals from late in the period of the Judean monarchy (compare bullae Nos. 147 and 152):[64]

38

(Belonging) to Berekhyahu	**[ל]ברכיהו**
son of Shemaʿyahu	**[בן ש]מעיהו**

The script is fine. The beginning of each line is missing. For the name *Berekhyahu*, see above, bulla No. 9. The name *Shemaʿyahu* is common in the Bible, on seals, among our bullae and in the Arad inscriptions (27: 2; 31: 5).

39–40. Gaʿali son of ʾElisamak

This person possessed two seals, from each of which one bulla was found:

39. This impression is well preserved, showing traces of a double linear frame and a double line dividing the two lines of fine script:

(Belonging) to Gaʿali	**לגעלי ב**
son of ʾElisamakh	**ן אליסמך**

39

The name *Gaʿali* is new to us, though in the Bible Gaal the son of Ebed is mentioned as the head of a

62 Avigad 1978b.
63 Avigad 1975, p. 69: 10; Bordreuil-Lemaire 1982, p. 30: 12.
64 See Avigad 1981, p. 303, Pl. נו: 1, for the apparent origin of the "bud" motif.

band who joined the Shechemites in their war against Abimelech (Judges 9: 26ff.). The name may be interpreted as deriving from *juʿal* in Arabic, meaning "scarab".[65] In the Bible, the name *ʾElisamakh* is found, though the form Semachaiah does appear. The full spelling here, with *yod*, is noteworthy. Compare also the following bulla, with the same name but in defective spelling.

40

40. This complete bulla has a two-line inscription divided by a double line terminating on the left in a vertical, curved line; within the curve is a sign consisting of two crossed lines. A similar arrangement had apparently existed on the right, off the present impression. The inscription is essentially identical to that of the previous bulla:

(Belonging) to Gaʿali	**לגעלי ב**
son of ʾEl(i)samakh	**ן אלסמך**

For the name *Gaʿali*, see above. The name *ʾElisamakh* is written here in a defective spelling, without *yod*, in contrast to the previous bulla which supplies us with the correct reading. The *nun* at the beginning of the second line is partly effaced. The top of the *mem* is blurred.

41. Gedalyahu (son of) Hoshaʿyahu

This broken bulla is composed of two fragments, each in a different collection; one portion is missing altogether. It has a linear frame and a ladder pattern divides the two-line inscription:

(Belonging) to Gedalyahu	**לגד[לי]הו**
(son of) Hoshaʿyahu	**הו[ש]עיהו**

The vulgar and careless script — most unusual in our bullae — is that of an unskilled scribe. The penultimate letter in the last line, *he*, has only two horizontal strokes, and is probably an accidental form. In the first name, Gedalyahu, the two middle letters are missing, while in the second name, the *shin* is missing.

41

65 Noth, p. 230.

42. Demalyahu son of Rapha᾿

Three identical bullae from this seal are in different states of preservation. Bulla No. 42a is the most complete, with the entire inscription. Bullae Nos. 42b and c are partly broken and the second line of the inscription is damaged; but the branch motif at the end of the inscription is better preserved. There is a linear frame and two lines divide the two-line inscription:

(Belonging) to Demalyahu	**לדמליהו**
son of Rapha᾿	**בן רפא**

42 a 42b 42c

The script is large and somewhat clumsy. The *dalet* and *he*, with the upper stroke extending far to the right, and the *mem* with a very short head are noteworthy.

The name *Demalyahu*, which also appears on bullae Nos. 43–45, is known from a seal: *ldmlyhw bn nryhw*.[66] The name would also seem to appear in the Bible, though in a wrongly spelled form (Remaliah, the *dalet* having been mistaken for a *resh*; 2 Kings 15: 25 etc.). On seals, parallel forms are also common: *dml᾿l*, *dml᾿*. The name Demalyahu consists of three components: the imperative form of the verb *dmm*, the preposition *lamed*, and the theophoric element, forming the verbal sentence *dom le-yahu*, "Stand still before Yahweh".[67]

Compare also the passage: "Be still before the Lord (*dwm lyhwh*), and wait patiently for him" (Psalms 37: 7). The name *Rapha᾿* also appears in the Bible (1 Chronicles 4: 12), a short form of the name Repha᾿yahu, which occurs on bullae Nos. 111 and 112. Rapha᾿ also appears on an Ammonite/Moabite seal[68] and in the Samaria Ostraca (24: 2).

43–46. Demalyahu son of Hosha῾yahu

This person possessed four seals, differing from one another in minor details.

43. Two bullae are impressed with this seal, one complete and the other partly

66 Diringer, No. 19.

67 For a discussion of this type of name, see B. Porten: "Domla᾿el and Related Names", *IEJ* 21 (1971), pp. 47ff.

68 Bordreuil-Lemaire 1976, p. 52, where this seal is defined as Hebrew.

43a

43b

44

45

46

broken. They have a linear frame, and the two-line inscription is divided by a double line:

(Belonging) to Demalyahu לדמליהו [ב]
son of Hoshaʿyahu ן הושעיה[ו]

The tiny script is fine. For the name *Demalyahu*, see above, bulla No. 42. The name *Hoshaʿyahu* is also found on other bullae.

44. This bulla is broken on the upper left. The impression resembles No. 43, but is from another seal. The upper register is narrower than the lower one:

(Belonging) to Demalyahu [לד]מליהו
son of Hoshaʿyahu [בן ה]ושעיהו

The first two letters in the upper line are missing, while the first three letters in the second line are blurred.

45. Only the right part of this bulla is preserved, bearing the first two letters of the first line and four letters of the second line. The seal resembled that of No. 43, above:

(Belonging) to Demalyahu לד[מליהו]
son of Hoshaʿyahu בן הו[שעיהו]

46. This bulla is broken on the left; a linear frame encloses a two-line inscription divided by a double line:

(Belonging) to Demalyahu לדמלי[הו]
(son of) Hoshaʿyahu הוש[עיהו]

The script is large and crude; apparently no room remained for the word *bn*. In the first name, we may note the ligature of *mem* and *yod*, with an intervening *lamed*. The *he* at the beginning of the second line extends beyond the frame.

47. Hoshaʿyahu (son of) Ḥeleṣyahu

Two impressions of this seal have been found, one a complete bulla and the other broken in the lower part. The complete bulla measures 14×10 mm. There is a linear frame enclosing three registers separated by double lines. In the upper register there is a Phoenician palmette motif (compare bulla No. 6), while the other two registers contain the inscription:

(Belonging) to Hoshaʿyahu	להושעיהו
(son of) Ḥeleṣyahu	חלציהו

47a

47b

The script is slightly blurred. The name *Hoshaʿyahu* is common in the assemblage and on seals. The name *Ḥeleṣyahu* is also found on bullae Nos. 79 and 157, and it is known on seals. In the Bible, the short form of this name, Helez, is mentioned. The name means "Yahweh has rescued". Compare also the Phoenician name *ḥlṣbʿl*.[69]

48. Hoshaʿyahu (son of) Shemaʿ

This is a large bulla bearing a small impression (6×9 mm). It bears a linear frame containing a two-line inscription divided by two lines:

(Belonging) to Hoshaʿyahu	להושעיהו
(son of) Shemaʿ	שמע

48

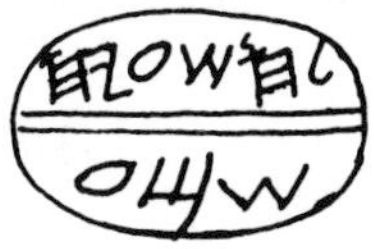

The inscription is complete (the bulla was difficult to photograph because of the depth of the impression). For the name *Hoshaʿyahu*, see above. The name *Shemaʿ* is a short form of Shemayahu, common in the Bible and on seals, but in our assemblage it appears only on this bulla.

69 F. L. Benz: *Personal Names in the Phoenician and Punic Inscriptions*, Rome 1972, pp. 110, 311.

49. Hiṣṣilyahu so of Shebanyahu

Of the two identical bullae, No. 49a is the better preserved. The impression measures 11×9 mm and has a linear frame enclosing a two-line inscription divided by two lines:

(Belonging) to Hiṣṣilyahu	**להצליהו**
son of Shebanyahu	**בן שבניהו**

49 a

49 b

The script is small and fine. The name *Hiṣṣilyahu*, which also appears on bullae Nos. 128 and 168, is not mentioned in the Bible but is found on seals and in the Lachish Letters (1: 1). It means "Yahweh has rescued". In the Ammonite bottle inscription there is a variant form, *hṣlʾl*. The name *Shebanyahu* is common in the Bible and on seals, and occurs on three other bullae of our assemblage. It is interpreted as *Shub-na-yahu*, meaning "Pray turn, O Yahweh."

50. Zakkur son of Neriyahu

50

This bulla is complete and the script is well preserved. The impression measures 12×10 mm. A groove around the edges of the impression indicates that the seal had been set in a thick bezel of metal. The two-line inscription is divided by a triple line:

(Belonging) to Zakkur son of	**לזכר בן**
Neriyahu	**נריהו**

The script is fine. The name *Zakkur*, a short form of Zekharyahu, is found in the Bible and on seals. *Neriyahu* is very common on the bullae of our assemblage.

51. Zakkur son of . . . yahu

51

This bulla is broken on the right side. The two-line inscription is divided by a double line:

(Belonging) to Zakkur son of [לז]כר בן
. . . yahu ...יהו

The letters in the first line are large. The tall *resh* with small head, and the crossing of the letters of the word *bn*, are noteworthy. Of the name *Zakkur*, only the last two letters remain, but the reconstruction is quite certain. See also the previous bulla. Of the patronymic, only the theophoric element has survived; and thus the seal might have belonged to the same person as No. 50.

52. Ḥubbaʾ son of Mattan

This bulla is broken at the bottom, but the small impression is intact. It measures 8 mm in diameter. A double linear frame containing a row of beads encloses a two-line inscription divided by a double line:

(Belonging) to Ḥubbaʾ לחבא ב
son of Mattan ן מתן

The tiny script is fine. The name *Ḥubba*ʾ, meaning to hide or conceal something, is a short form of the theophoric name אליחבא (2 Samuel 23: 32; 1 Chronicles 11: 33), meaning "Yahweh shall conceal, protect (the newly born infant)." The same element *ḥb*ʾ is found in the Bible, spelled with a *he* rather than an *aleph*, in the name Ḥabaiah (Ezra 2 61; Nehemiah 7: 63), and in the shorter form Ḥubbah (*Ketib*: Yeḥubbah; 1 Chronicles 7: 34). Thus, the name on our bulla is to be pronounced Ḥubbaʾ (though if taken as the Qal form, it would be Ḥabbaʾ, a hypocoristic form of Ḥabaiah). *Mattan*, the short form of Mattanyahu, is common and is found on several other bullae of our assemblage.

52

53–54. Ḥagab son of Ṣephanyahu

This person possessed two identical seals, differing only in the size of the letters. Four bullae have been found.

53a

53b

53. Of this seal there are two bullae, one (No. 53a), almost complete, with an impression 12 mm long; and the other (No. 53b), surviving only in its lower part. The outer linear frame encloses a two-line inscription divided by two lines:

(Belonging) to Ḥagab son of Ṣephanyahu — **לחגב בן / צפניהו**

The script is fine. The name *Ḥagab* meaning "locust, grasshopper", is found in the Bible. In the Books of Ezra and Nehemiah, it is mentioned as the name of a family (variant: Hagabah) which had returned from Exile. The Lachish Letters (1: 3) mention Ḥagab son of Yaʾazanyahu. The word *gbh*, a synonym for "locust", appears on a Hebrew seal which also bears a locust motif.[70] For the use of the names of insects as personal names, see also a seal which bears the name Parʿosh, meaning flea.[71] *Ṣephanyahu* occurs in the Bible as the name of a prophet, and is common on seals.

54. This seal, too, was impressed on two bullae:

(Belonging) to Ḥagab son of Ṣephanyahu — **לחגב בן / צפני[הו]**

The letters of this seal are slightly smaller than those of bulla No. 53. Bulla No. 54a is fired black and lacks the two last letters of its inscription. Bulla No. 54b is broken in the lower right corner. The script is blurred.

54a

55. Ḥaggi son of Hoduyahu

This bulla is broken on the right edge. The two-line inscription is divided by a ladder pattern:

(Belonging) to Ḥaggi son of Hoduyahu — **[ל]חגי בן / הודויהו**

The letters are large. Of special interest is the *dalet*

54b

70 Avigad 1966, pp. 50–53.
71 Vattioni 1978, No. 354.

in the second line, the upper stroke of which extends to the right in an emphatic manner.

The name *Ḥaggi* is vocalized in the Bible (MT) in two manners: חַגִּי (in the First Temple period) and חַגַּי (the name of the prophet, in the period of the Babylonian Exile). The name is common on seals and has recently been discovered on the seal of an official: *bnyhw nʿr ḥgy*.[72] The name *Hoduyahu* is vocalized in the Bible as הוֹדַוְיָהוּ, but it may well be preferable to vocalize it הוֹדוּיָהוּ, as in the Septuagint, in the jussive plural meaning "Thank Yahweh." This name also appears in the Lachish Letters (3: 17), on an unpublished seal, and in the Elephantine Papyri, in the shorter form Hoduyah.[73] See also bulla No. 117.

55

56. Ḥaṭṭush (son of) Shephaṭyahu

There are three bullae impressed with this seal, in varying states of preservation. Bulla No. 56a bears a complete impression, 11 mm long. Bulla No. 56b lacks several letters in the second line; bulla No. 56c is merely a small upper fragment with the name in the upper line. A double linear frame encloses the two-line inscription which is divided by a double line:

(Belonging) to Ḥaṭṭush	לחטש
(son of) Shephaṭyahu	שפטיהו

Ḥaṭṭush apparently represents a name mentioned in the later books of the Bible (Ezra 8: 2; Nehemiah 3: 10ff.). Several persons of this name were among those who returned from Exile in the Persian period. It also appears on Ammonite seals.[74] The meaning of the name is unknown. The name *Shephaṭyahu* is common in the Bible, on seals and among the bullae of our assemblage.

56a

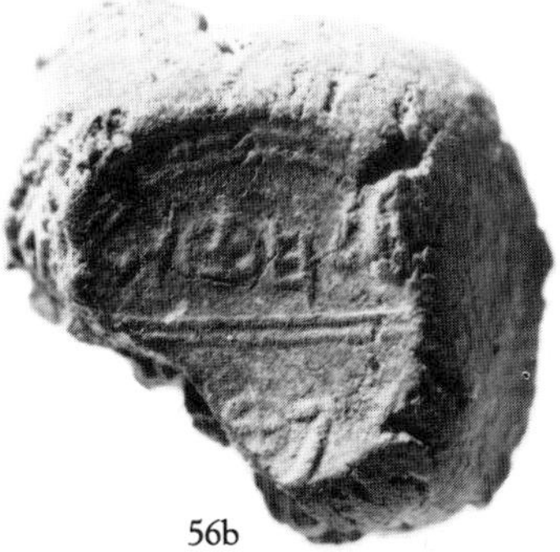

56b

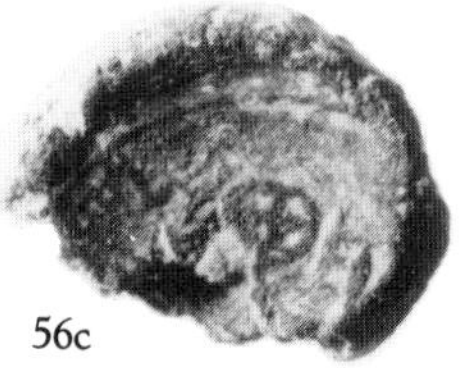

56c

72 Avigad 1976c, Fig. 12: 3.
73 Cowley, Nos. 2: 2, 19; 10, etc.
74 Avigad 1970, p. 287: 3; P. Bordreuil, *Syria* 50 (1973), p. 187.

57

57. Ḥeleq son of ʾEzer

This bulla is complete, measuring 14×16 mm. The clay is fired black. A linear frame encloses a two-line inscription divided by two curved lines:

(Belonging) to Ḥeleq	**לחלק ב**
son of ʾEzer	**ן עזר**

The name *Ḥeleq* is mentioned in the Bible: a person of this name was among the Gileadites, and another was among the family heads of Manasseh (Numbers 26: 30; Joshua 17: 2). The name also appears on seals and in the Samaria Ostraca (Nos. 22–27). It is also the name of a district named after the clan noted above. As a personal name, it is undoubtedly shortened from a theophoric name such as Hilqiyahu. *ʾEzer* is a very common name.

58

58. Ḥilqiyahu son of . . . yahu

This bulla is broken. It is divided into three registers by two double lines. In the upper register there is a Phoenician palmette (compare bulla No. 6). The inscription is in the two lower registers, though most of the script in the lower register has been lost:

(Belonging) to Ḥilqiyahu	**לחלקיהו ב**
(son of) . . . . yahu	**[ן] ....יהו**

The script is fine. *Ḥilqiyahu* is the name of several important figures in the Bible, such as a high priest, the father of Eliakim and the father of Jeremiah; it also appears on seals and among the bullae of our assemblage. Only traces of the second name on this bulla survive.

59

59. Ḥilqiyahu son of . . .

This complete bulla, measuring 16×19 mm, is fired black. The impression measures 15×11 mm. The linear frame encloses a two-line inscription divided by a double line:

(Belonging) to Ḥilqiyahu	**לחלקיהו**
son of	**בן ....**

The script is very blurred. In the second line, traces of the word *bn* can just be discerned.

60

60. Ḥeleṣ son of ʾAḥʾab

This bulla is damaged on three edges. The two-line inscription is divided by a double line, and there are pellets in the field:

(Belonging) to Ḥeleṣ son of ʾAḥʾab	[ל]חלץ בנ[ן] אחאב

The beginning and end of the first line are damaged. *Ḥeleṣ* is the hypocoristic form of the full name Ḥeleṣyahu, appearing on bullae Nos. 47, 79 and 154. It is found in the Bible (2 Samuel 23: 26; 1 Chronicles 2: 39; 27: 10), on Samaria Ostraca (Nos. 22, 26, etc.) and in Phoenician inscriptions.[75] The name *ʾAḥʾab* is very common among the bullae of our assemblage.

61

61. Ḥananyahu (son of) Neḥemyahu

This bulla is complete. The round impression measures 11 mm in diameter. The two-line inscription is divided by two lines:

(Belonging) to Ḥananyahu (son of) Neḥemyahu	לחנניהו נחמי[הו]

The script is careless. The final letters in the second line are blurred. The name *Ḥananyahu* is common in the Bible, on seals and among the bullae of our assemblage. The name *Neḥemyahu* is known in the Bible only in its shorter form Nehemiah. Though the final letters of the inscription are blurred, the reconstruction of this name has been restored in a full form, in keeping with the spelling found on seals.

62. Ḥananyahu (son of) Zeraḥ

This bulla is almost complete. The round impression measures 9 mm in diameter. The linear

75 Benz, *op. cit.* (above, n. 69), pp. 109, 311.

62

frame encloses a two-line inscription divided by two lines:

(Belonging) to Ḥananyahu חנניהו
(son of) Zeraḥ זרח

In the first name, *Ḥananyahu*, the upper part of the *ḥet* and the end of the name are not clearly visible in the photograph. The second name, *Zeraḥ*, is somewhat problematic. It apparently begins with the letter *ṣade*, but *ṣrḥ* is an unlikely name. On the other hand, there is sometimes a close resemblance between the forms of the letters *ṣade* and *zayin* (see, for example, the *zayin* on bulla No. 71, which closely resembles a *ṣade*). Thus, the engraver, who was not a skilled craftsman, probably had in mind the letter *zayin*. The name Zeraḥ is new on seals, though it is very common in the Bible. Note also the full form, Yehozeraḥ, on bulla No. 118.

63. Ḥanan son of ʿUzziyahu son of . . .

63

This bulla is damaged. The surface is divided into three registers by two double lines. The lower register is entirely missing in the impression:

(Belonging) to Ḥanan son of [לח]נן בן
ʿUzziyahu son of [ע]זיהו בן
. . . .

The script is fine. Both names lack the first letter. The name *Ḥanan* is the shortened form of Ḥananyahu and is very common. The name *ʿUzziyahu*, here in a defective spelling without the first *waw*, is also common in the Bible and on seals. The name of the grandfather is missing.

64. Ḥanan son of Shemaʿyahu

64

This bulla is broken on the upper left. The linear frame encloses a two-line inscription divided by a double line:

(Belonging) to Ḥanan son of [ל]חנן בן
Shemaʿyahu שמעיהו

The script is fine. Both names here are common.

65. Ṭobiyahu (son of) ʿAbdaʾ

This bulla, the impression of which is incomplete, has a linear frame and a two-line inscription divided by a double line:

(Belonging) to Ṭobiyahu לטבי[הו]
(son of) ʿAbdaʾ עבדא

The letters are large. Note especially the large *ṭet*, the rhomboid *ʿayin*, the tall *dalet* and its ligature with the tail of the *bet* (the dot between these two letters is accidental, a flaw in the clay). The clear and blurred letters in the upper line make up the name *Ṭobiyahu*. See the discussion of this name above, bulla No. 14.

The name *ʿAbdaʾ* is a short form of ʿObadyahu. In Nehemiah 11: 17, we read of Abda the son of Shammua, a Levite leader in Jerusalem in the days of Nehemiah. The parallel passage in 1 Chronicles 9: 16 refers to the same person as Obadiah the son of Shemaiah. The name ʿAbdaʾ also appears in the Samaria Ostraca (57: 1) and is common on non-Hebrew seals.

65

66. Yaʾush son of ʾElishamaʿ

This bulla is complete. The impression measures 11×9 mm. The linear frame encloses a two-line inscription divided by a double line:

(Belonging) to Yaʾush son of ליאש בן
ʾElishamaʿ אלשמע

The fine script is clear. The two final letters of the inscription are damaged. For the name *Yaʾush*, see the discussion above, bulla No. 30. For the name ʾElishamaʿ, see bulla No. 4.

66

67. Yaʾush son of Pedayahu

This bulla is broken on the lower edge. The linear frame encloses a two-line inscription divided by a double line:

(Belonging) to Yaʾush ליאש
son of Pedayahu [ב]ן פדיהו

Most of the letters in the lower line are damaged,

67

but the proposed reading is certain. For the name *Yaʾush*, see above. For the name *Pedayahu*, see bulla No. 99.

68. Yedaʿyahu son of Karmi

There are two fragmentary bullae impressed with the same seal, complementing one another to yield the full inscription. The two-line inscription is divided by three horizontal lines. Bulla No. 68a bears the first three letters of each line, while bulla No. 68b lacks the first two letters in each line:

(Belonging) to Yedaʿyahu	**(a) לידן] + (b)]ידעיהו = לידעיהו**
son of Karmi	**בן כֿ]]כרמי = בן כרמי**

68b

68a

The name *Yedaʾyahu* (Jedaiah) is common in the Bible. Several heads of priestly families by this name were among those who returned from Exile. It is also found in the Arad Inscriptions (31: 7 and others) and appears on a seal. The element *ydʿ* is a component in other theophoric names, such as *yhwydʿ*, *ʾlydʿ* and the like. The name *Karmi*, from the biblical Hebrew word for vineyard, is found on a stamped jar-handle from Lachish.[76] In the Bible it occurs as the name of a son of Reuben (Genesis 46: 9) and of Judah (Chronicles 4: 1).

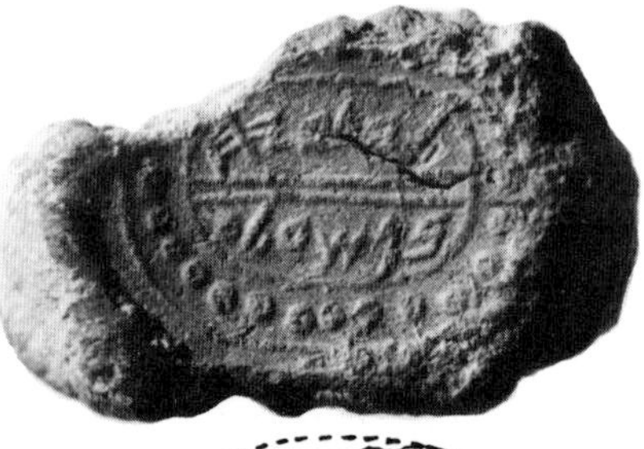

69

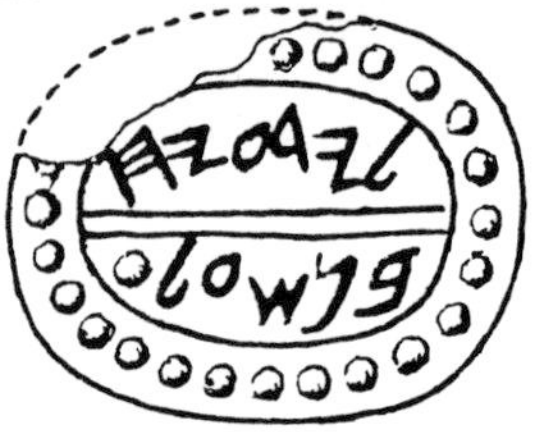

69. Yedaʿyahu son of Shuʿal

This bulla is broken on the upper left. It is 19 mm long, and has a double linear frame containing a row of beads (as on bullae Nos. 52 and 83), a border motif common on Hebrew seals. The two-line inscription is divided by a double line:

(Belonging) to Yedaʿyahu	**לידעיהו**
son of Shuʿal	**בן שעל ·**

The script is fine. The inscription is followed by a pellet. For the name *Yedaʿyahu*, see above. The name *Shuʿal*, literally meaning "fox", is found in

76 O. Tufnell: *Lachish* III, London 1953, p. 341, Pl. 47: B, 7.

the Bible,[77] on seals[78] and on several other bullae. It also appears in the Arad Inscriptions (49: 14; 38: 2) and on a jar-handle.[79] Note also the land of Shual (1 Samuel 13: 17) and Hazar-shual (Joshua 15: 28).

70. Yehuʾ son of *Mšmš*

This complete bulla is 16 mm long. It has a double linear frame enclosing a three-line inscription divided by two arched, double lines which terminate in rosette-like motifs. The second line of the inscription, containing the letters *bn*, is located within the two resulting triangles at each side (compare bulla No. 31).

70

(Belonging) to Yehuʾ	ליהוא
son of	ב ן
Mšmš	משמש

The script is fine. The name *Yehuʾ*, new on seals, is mentioned in the Bible, *inter alia*, as the name of Jehu, king of Israel (2 Kings 9: 2, etc.) and of Jehu the prophet (1 Kings 16: 1, 7 etc.). The patronymic *Mšmš* is new, though it appears on another Hebrew seal, as yet unpublished. It may in fact derive from a place name (compare the name *Prpr* on bulla No. 138). In Mishnaic Hebrew, *mšmš* means "to touch, examine, serve", etc. In Arabic, *mishmesh* means apricot.

71–73. Yehoʾaḥ (son of) ʾEliʿaz

This person possessed three seals, similar but not identical. One bulla from each seal has been found.

71. This bulla is damaged on the edges, but the impression is complete. The linear frame encloses a two-line inscription divided by a double line:

(Belonging) to Yehoʾaḥ	ליהואח
(son of) ʾEliʿaz	אליעז

71

The script is fine. The *waw* in the first name has been crowded in between the *he* and the *aleph*, probably as an afterthought.

77 *Enṣ. Miqr.* IV, col. 569 (Hebrew).
78 Diringer, No. 41 (*lšʿl bn ʾlyšʿ*); Bordreuil-Lemaire 1976, p. 51:17 (*lʾlyšb bn šʿl*).
79 N. Avigad: *IEJ* 22 (1972), pp. 5–9.

72

The name *Yeho'ah* is new; it inverts the components of the name 'Aḥiyahu. In the Bible the short form of this name, *yw'ḥ*, is found. The name *'Eli'az* has the vowel letter *yod*, in contrast to the defective spelling on bulla No. 72; compare also bulla No. 28. For the meaning of the name, see bulla No. 17.

72. This impression is as the above, but of a second seal. At the end of the inscription is a space filler in the form of a branch:

(Belonging) to Yeho'aḥ	**[ל]יהואח**
(son of) 'El(i)'az	**אלעז**

For these names, see above; but note the defective spelling of the second name, in contrasr to No. 71.

73

73. This bulla is damaged on the right edge; the impression resembles the above, but is of a third seal:

(Belonging) to Yeho'aḥ	**[ליה]ואח ב**
son of 'El(i)'az	**[ן] אלעז**

In contrast to the cursive script of the two above seals, here the letters are large, thick and upright, resembling a lapidary script. In the first line the first three letters are missing, while in the second line the first letter is missing. On this seal, we may note the addition of the word *bn*, "son", whereas the branch motif is omitted.

74. Yeho'az son of Mattan

74a

74b

There are two bullae, one complete (the impression measures 9.5×7 mm), and the other broken into two fragments. The double linear frame encloses a two-line inscription divided by a double line. At the end of each line of script is a branch, serving as a space filler:

(Belonging) to Yeho'az	**ליהועז**
son of Mattan	**בן מתן**

The script is fine. The name *Yeho'az*, reversing the components of the name 'Uzziyahu, is not found in the Bible. It is found on seals and in the Arad Inscriptions (31: 3). Compare also the name

ʾEliʿaz on bullae Nos. 28 and 71. *Mattan* is the short form of the name Mattanyahu and is very common in the Bible, on seals and among the bullae of our assemblage.

75. Yeqamyahu son of Meshullam

There are three identical bullae: two of them complete (Nos. 75a and b), and the third a fragment bearing only the upper line of the inscription (No. 75c). The two-line inscription is divided by a double line. At the bottom there is a Phoenician palmette motif (compare bullae No. 6):

(Belonging) to Yeqamyahu	**ליקמיהו**
son of Meshullam	**בן משלם**

The script is fine. The biblical name *Yeqamyahu* is common on seals and in the Arad Inscriptions (39: 1, 2: 59 etc.). *Meshullam*, here written defectively without the *waw*, is a short form of Meshelemyahu. It is very common in the Bible and is also found on seals, in the Elephantine Papyri and among the bullae of our assemblage.

75 a

75b

75c

76. Yeqamyahu ....

The left part of this bulla is missing. A double linear frame encloses a two-line inscription divided by a double line:

(Belonging) to Yeqamyahu	**ליקמ[יהו]**
(son of) s...	**ס...**

Only the first three and a half letters of the first line have been preserved, as well as one letter in the lower line. This seal of Yeqamyahu differs from that of Yeqamyahu son of Meshullam, and it was apparently of another person. The letter at the beginning of the second line seems to be a *samekh*.

76

77

77. Yeqamyahu son of Naḥum

This bulla is complete. The impression measures 14×11 mm. A linear frame encloses the large figure of a man facing right with one arm stretched out before him. The figure is dressed in a long robe ornamented schematically by two bands of stripes. Human figures appear on only two bullae of our assemblage. Figures of devotees are quite common in the iconography of West Semitic seals, and they occasionally also appear on Hebrew seals. Flanking the figure are two vertical lines of script:

(Belonging) to Yeqamyahu	**ליקמיהו**
son of Naḥum	**בן נחם**

The letters are large and slightly clumsy. For the name *Yeqamyahu*, see bulla No. 75. The name *Naḥum* is common.

78. Yirmeyahu (son of) Yishmaᶜᵓel

This bulla is broken on the left and above. The linear frame encloses a two-line inscription divided by two lines:

(Belonging) to Yirmeyahu	**לירמ̇[יהו]**
(son of) Yishmaᶜᵓel	**ישמעא̇[ל]**

78

The letters are large. In the first line, only the first three and a half letters are preserved, and the proposed reconstruction, *Yirmeyahu*, is the most likely, though other names, such as *yrmwt* or *yrmy*, are possible. This is apparently the only bulla of our assemblage bearing the name Jeremiah. This name is known, of course, in the Bible — not only as the name of the prophet but also as that of several other persons, eight of them contemporaries of the prophet. It is also common on seals and in the Arad Inscriptions (24: 15–16). The name *Yishmaᶜᵓel* is very common among the bullae of our assemblage.

79. Yishmaᶜᵓel son of Shuᶜal son of Ḥeleṣyahu

This bulla is almost complete. It is divided into three registers by two double lines. The script is somewhat careless and some of the letters are damaged:

(Belonging) to Yishmaʾel לישמעאל
son of Shuʿal son of [ב]ן שעל בן
Ḥelesyahu [חל]ציה[ו]

The biblical name *Yishmaʿʾel* is very common among the bullae of our assemblage, occurring in nine instances. For the name *Shuʿal*, see bulla No. 69. *Ḥeleṣyahu* is the most likely reconstruction of the name in the final line. This name is found on two other bullae and is discussed under bulla No. 47. The present bulla is one of five in our assemblage noting three generations (see bulla No. 21).

79

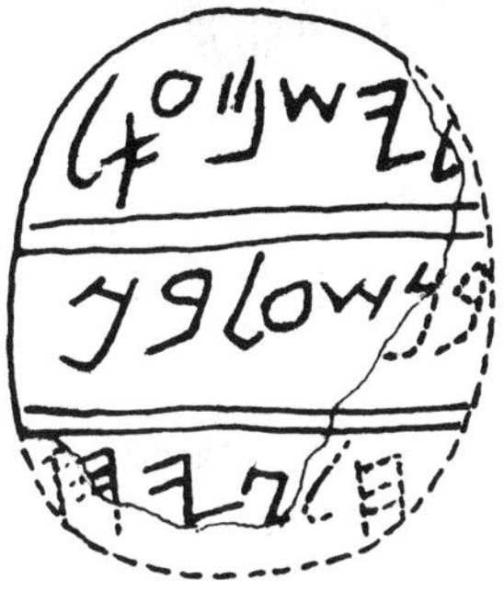

80. Yishmaʿʾel son of Maḥseyahu

This bulla is broken on several edges. The two-line inscription is divided by a ladder pattern:

(Belonging) to Yishmaʿʾel לישמ[עאל]
son of Maḥseyahu [ב]ן מחסי[הו]

In the first line, only the first four letters survive, and the name as restored is certainly reasonable. In the second line the script is blurred, but the first three letters of the name, *mḥs*, enable the proposed reconstruction. For the name *Maḥseyahu*, see below, bulla No. 85.

80

81. Yishmaʿʾel . . . .

This bulla is damaged. The two-line inscription is divided by two lines:

(Belonging) to Yishmaʿʾel לישמ[עאל]
. . . .

The script is large, careless and blurred. In the first line three or four letters are preserved. The most likely reconstruction is as proposed, Yishmaʿʾel. In the second line, traces of letters are difficult to decipher, but possibly read *bn p*. . . .

81

82. Yishmaʿʾel . . . . .

This is the upper fragment of a bulla, bearing only the first line of a two-line inscription, with traces of a dividing line below:

82

(Belonging) to Yishma

(Belonging) to Yishmaʿʾel **לישמ[עאל]**

....

The letters are large. The most likely reconstruction of the name in the upper line is Yishmaʿʾel.

83. Yishaʿyahu son of Ḥamal

This complete bulla measures 15×17 mm. A deep groove surrounding the impression indicates that the seal-stone had been set in a bezel. The round impression is 11 mm in diameter. The clay is fired black. The double linear frame, containing a row of beads common on Hebrew seals, encloses a two-line inscription divided by a double line:

(Belonging) to Yishaʿyahu **לישעיהו**
son of Ḥamal **בן חמל**

83

obverse

reverse

The script is tiny and fine, but slightly blurred. The name *Yishaʿyahu* is known in the Bible as that of the prophet Isaiah the son of Amoz, as well as of several other persons. It is also common on seals. The name *Ḥamal* is also known on a seal: *ldršyhw/ḥml*.[80] It is a short form of a theophoric name such as *Ḥamalyahu, in the past tense Qal form of the verb *ḥml*, meaning "Yahweh has pitied". In the Bible, a name of this root appears in the Paʿul form: *ḥmwl* (Genesis 46: 12; 1 Chronicles 20: 5). Compare also the imperfect forms *yḥmlyh* on a seal[81] and *yḥml* on a pottery decanter.[82]

80 Avigad 1975, p. 69: 14; Diringer, No. 51.
81 Avigad 1975, p. 69: 14; Diringer, No. 51.
82 W. G. Dever: "Iron Age Epigraphic Material from the Area of Khirbet el-Kom", *Hebrew Union College Annual* 40/41 (1969/70), pp. 169–170.

84. Yishaʿyahu (son of) ʾEliṣedeq

This bulla is broken. The two-line inscription is divided by a double line:

(Belonging) to Yishaʿyahu	**[לי]שעיהו**
(son of) ʾEliṣedeq	**[א]לצד[ק]**

The somewhat careless script is blurred and damaged. Despite the blurring, the letters as proposed above can be discerned; thus in the first line is restored the name *Yishaʿyahu*, and in the second line the name *ʾEliṣedeq*. The latter name is new and is based on the example of the biblical name Yehoṣadaq.

84

85. Maḥseyahu (son of) ʾEliyahu

This bulla is broken in the lower left corner, but the inscription is complete. It is 12 mm long. The two-line inscription is divided by two lines:

(Belonging) to Maḥseyahu	**למחסיהו**
(son of) ʾEliyahu	**אליהו**

The script is fine. The name *Maḥseyahu* appears in the Bible in the shorter form Mahseiah as the name of the grandfather of Baruch the scribe (Jeremiah 32: 12) and of Seraiah his brother (Jeremiah 52: 59). The meaning of the name is "Yahweh is a refuge, cover". Compare Psalms 91: 2: "... say to the Lord, 'My refuge (*mḥsy*) and my fortress; my God, in whom I trust". This name was quite common among the Jews of Elephantine,[83] and it also appears in the Arad Inscriptions (23: 6). See also the following bulla. For the name *ʾEliyahu*, see bulla No. 27.

85

86. Maḥseyahu son of Pelaṭyahu

This complete bulla is 18 mm long; the impression measures 12×11 mm. The linear frame encloses a two line inscription divided by a double line:

(Belonging) to Maḥseyahu	**למח[סי]הו**
son of Pelaṭyahu	**בן פלטיהו**

86

83 Cowley, Nos. 6: 22, 8: 29, 9: 18, etc.

For the name *Mahseyahu*, see the previous bulla. *Pelatyahu* is one of the common names in our assemblage; it is borne by six persons. In the Bible, where the name appears only in the later books, it is vocalized פְּלַטְיָהוּ or in the shorter form פְּלַטְיָה. It is also found on seals and in the Elephantine Papyri.[84] It means "Yahweh has rescued".

87. Maʿaśeyahu (son of) Miʾamen

This bulla is broken on the right. The linear frame encloses a two-line inscription divided by a double line; there are two pellets above the upper line of script:

(Belonging) to Maʿaśeyahu	**[למע]שיהו**
(son of) Miʾamen	**מיאמן**

87

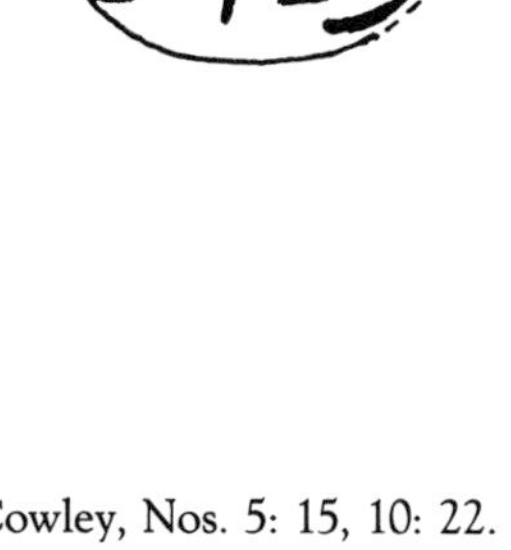

In the upper line, the first two letters of the name are missing, and the proposed reconstruction is likely but not certain. The name *myʾmn* is apparently to be vocalized *Miʾamen*; it is complete, though the first *mem* is slightly damaged. The peculiar form of the *aleph* has two horizontal strokes close together, high up the stem. This name is not mentioned in the Bible, but is found on a seal,[85] on a bulla from Lachish,[86] and apparently also on bulla No. 88. Another name with the same basic element (*ʾmn*) is *ywʾmn*, also on a seal.[87] The name Miʾamen might be interpreted as deriving from אָמֵן, אֵמוּן, "faithfulness, truth", in the same sense as the name Amon (king of Judah).[88] The name *ywʾmn* may have the meaning of the phrase *ʾlhyʾmn* in Isaiah 65: 16: "God of truth". If so, Miʾamen could be interpreted as an interrogative, of the same type as names like Micaiah or Michael. In this case, the two names based on this root, *myʾmn* and *ywʾmn*, would ask the question and answer it, respectively: "Who is of truth? Yahweh is of truth!"

84 Cowley, Nos. 5: 15, 10: 22.
85 Hestrin-Dayagi, No. 94.
86 Aharoni, *op. cit.* (above, n. 1), p. 21.
87 Avigad 1954, p. 151 (Hebrew).
88 *Ens. Miqr.* I, cols. 422–423 (Hebrew).

88. Mi'amen son of 'Ephai

This bulla lacks its right side. The linear frame encloses a two-line inscription divided by two lines:

(Belonging) to Mi'amen [למ]יאמן
son of 'Ephai [בן] עפי

88

In the upper line, the three final letters are very clear, preceded by the triangular head of a fourth letter, which we have interpreted as a *yod*. The two upper strokes of *yod* occasionally meet to form a triangle; compare bulla No. 11, in the name Yeqamyahu; bulla No. 39, in the name 'Elisamakh; bulla No. 49, in the name Hiṣṣilyahu; and bulla No. 147, in the name Pelaṭyahu. Thus, we have restored here the name *Mi'amen*, preserved completely on bulla No. 87. For its meaning, see above.

The name *'Ephai* seems to appear in the Bible in two different forms: 'Ophai (*ketib*) and 'Ephai (*qeri*), in Jeremiah 40: 8. The Septuagint prefers the former, which is also found in a Hebrew tomb inscription of the 7th century CE.[89] The "sons of Ephai the Netophathite" were contemporaries of Jeremiah and were among those "who had not been taken into exile" after the conquest of Jerusalem. The name is sometimes explained as deriving from the word *'wf*, "fowl".[90]

89. Merab (son of) Yishma''el

This bulla is broken at the bottom and partly damaged in its upper part. It measures 17 × 14 mm. The clay is baked grey-brown. The linear frame encloses a two-line inscription divided by two lines:

(Belonging) to Merab למיר[ב]
(son of) Yishma''el ישמעאל

89

Of the first name, only the first three letters (*myr*) have survived. The most likely restoration is that proposed, *myrb*. In the Bible, the name of *Merab*,

89 Dever, *op. cit.* (above, n. 82), p. 151.
90 Noth, p. 230; *Enṣ. Miqr.* VI, col. 215 (Hebrew).

daughter of Saul, is written without the medial vowel *yod* (1 Samuel 14: 59, etc.). In contrast, the full spelling of the name occurs on a seal: *lʾnyhw/myrb*,[91] where it is assumed that the name represents the patronymic. Similarly, the name on our bulla may well be in the masculine, for otherwise the designation *bt*, "daughter", as is generally found on women's seals, would surely have appeared. There are many names in the Bible which serve both sexes.[92] Compare the name ʿImmadiyahu, on bulla No. 93.

90

90. Mikhayahu son of ʾEl(i)ʿaz

This bulla is complete. The linear frame (11×13 mm) encloses a two-line inscription divided by a double line:

(Belonging) to Mikhayahu למכיהו
son of ʾEl(i)ʿaz בן אלעז

The script is fine. The name Mikhayahu is vocalized in the MT in two manners: מִיכָיָהוּ and מִכָיְהוּ. It appears on seven of our bullae. For ʾEl(i)ʿaz, see above, bulla No. 17, and others.

91

91. Mikhayahu (son of) Yeshaʿyahu

This bulla is complete, but pressure by the fingers from the sides while the clay was still soft have led to the blurring of several letters. The two-line inscription is divided by a double line:

(Belonging) to Mikhayahu למכיה[ו]
(son of) Yeshaʿyahu ישעי[הו]

For these names, see above.

92

92. Mikhayahu son of Meshullam

This is a complete bulla. The impression measures 9×10 mm. The linear frame encloses a two-line inscription divided by a double line:

(Belonging) to Mikhayahu למכיהו
son of Meshullam בן משלם

For the name *Mikhayahu*, see above. The name *Meshullam* appears on three other bullae of our assemblage, on seals, in the Arad Inscriptions (39:

91 Avigad 1982, pp. 59–62.
92 *Ens. Miqr.* VIII, cols. 44–45, s.v. *shemot ʿeṣem praṭiyim* (Hebrew).

3), in the Elephantine Papyri and frequently in the Bible, where it is vocalized as מְשֻׁלָּם. This name is a short form of Meshelemiah, meaning "Yahweh recompenses" (see also bulla No. 75).

93

93. Semakhyahu son of ʿImmadiyahu

This bulla is partly damaged, mainly on the right. There appears to be traces of a double linear frame enclosing the two-line inscription, which is divided by a triple line:

(Belonging) to Semakhyahu [לס]מכיה[ו]
son of ʿImmadiyahu בן עמדיה[ו]

We may note the fine script of this bulla, as well as the previous three. Here, in the first line only three complete letters (*mky*) remain. There is room for at least two letters to the right, and we therefore reconstruct the line to read: [*ls*]*mkyhw*. For the name *Semakhyahu*, see bulla No. 119. *ʿImmadiyahy* was first found on a seal, as a feminine name: *lʿmdyhw bt šbnyhw*.[93] Thus, we might assume that our ʿImmadiyahu was Semakhyahu's mother. In the Bible there are many instances in which a man is designated by his matronym, such as Joash the son of Seruiah, Jehozabad the son of Shimrith, Jozachar the son of Shimeath and others. So far, however, no seals or seal impressions have been found bearing the name of owners identified by their matronyms; in every case, it is the patronym which appears. It should be assumed that on this bulla, too, the name ʿImmadiyahu refers to the owner's father. We know of names in the Bible which served both sexes: Abijah, Maachah, Shelomith and the like. Quite recently, an ostracon was discovered in excavations at Ḥorvat ʿUzza in the Negev, containing a list of names, among which is *ʿmdyhw bn zkr*, ʿImmadiyahu son of Zakkur.[94] This surely proves the duality of the gender of this name; the same argument can be applied to the name Merab, discussed above, bulla No. 89. ʿImmadiyahu, meaning "Yahweh is with me", is parallelled by the biblical name ʿImmanuʾel, "God is with us" (Isaiah 7: 14); in the Elephantine Papyri we read the name *ʿmnyh* (ʿImmanuyah), meaning "Yahweh is with us".[95]

93 Diringer, No. 61.
94 See, recently, ʿImmadiyahu son of Zakkur, on an ostracon; I. Beit-Arieh: "The Ostracon of Aḥiqam from Ḥorvat ʿUzza", *EI* 18 (1985), p. 94 (Hebrew; English summary on pp. 68*–69*), where the name *ʿmdyhw* is vocalized, unconvincingly, as *ʿAmadyahu*.
95 Cowley, No. 22: 105.

94

94. Mikhayahu (son of) Pelaṭyahu

This bulla is complete; its edges are poorly formed. The two-line inscription is divided by two lines:

(Belonging) to Mikhayahu **למכי[הו]**
(son of) Pelaṭyahu **פלטיהו**

In the first line it is difficult to discern the two final letters of the name *Mikhayahu*. For the name *Pelaṭyahu*, see bulla No. 86.

95. Mikhayahu son of Shaḥar

The left side of this bulla is missing. The two-line inscription is divided by two lines:

(Belonging) to Mikhayahu **למכי[הו] ב**
son of Shaḥar **ן שח[ר]**

The script is large and clumsy. The names can be restored with certainty. For *Mikhayahu*, see above. For the name *Shaḥar*, see bullae Nos. 22–23.

95

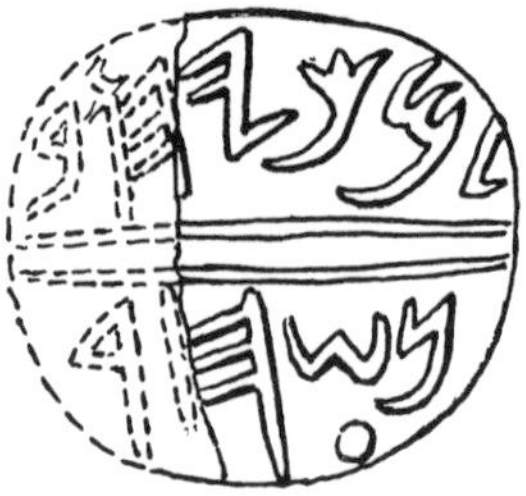

96–97. Mikhayahu (son of) Shebanyahu

This person possessed two very similar but not identical seals. A single bulla of each seal was found.

96. This bulla is complete. The linear frame encloses a two-line inscription divided by two lines, bearing three pellets:

(Belonging) to Mikhayahu **למכיהו**
(son of) Shebanyahu **שבניהו**

96

97

For the first, see above. For the second name, see bulla No. 49.

97. This bulla is complete. The frame is of a ladder pattern, enclosing a two-line inscription divided by a double line:

(Belonging) to Mikhayahu	**למכיהו**
(son of) Shebanyahu	**שבניהו**

The script is crude and clumsy. Some of the letters are blurred, but the reading is certain. For the names, see above. This is the last of the group of seven bullae bearing the name Mikhayahu.

98

98. Malkiyahu (son of) Ḥeleq

This bulla, broken on the right, is 17 mm long. It is divided into three registers by two double lines. In the upper register is a very schematic rendering of a fish, a motif found on several Hebrew seals. The two-line inscription occupies the two lower registers:

(Belonging) to Malkiyahu	**[ל]מלכיהו**
(son of) Ḥeleq	**חלק**

The name *Malkiyahu* is known in the Bible and on seals, and appears on several of our bullae. For the name Ḥeleq, see bulla No. 57.

99. Malkiyahu son of Pedayahu

This bulla is complete. The two-line inscription is divided by two arched lines terminating in pellets, with triangles between them:

(Belonging) to Malkiyahu	**למלכיהו**
son of Pedayahu	**בן פריהו**

99

For the first name, see above. The full name *Pedayahu*, occurring on three more of our bullae, appears once in the Bible (1 Chronicles 27: 2); its shorter form, lacking the final *waw*, is more common. It also appears on seals and in the Arad Inscriptions (49: 15). Other names using the verb *pdh* include *pdʾl*, *pdhʾl* and *pdhṣwr*. The name means "Yahweh has redeemed".

100

100. Menaḥem (son of) Ḥananyahu

This bulla is damaged. There is a wide margin on the left. The two-line inscription is divided by two lines:

(Belonging) to Menaḥem	**[ל]מנחם**
(son of) Ḥananyahu	**חנניהו**

The inscription is very blurred, but several letters can be discerned and the others can be restored as proposed. Both names are common.

101-102. Menaḥem son of Yishmaʿʾel

This person possessed two identical seals, with only minor differences between them, in the letter shapes and the dividing lines.

101. This is a broken bulla; the two fragments have been joined in the photograph. The linear frame encloses a two-line inscription divided by a double line:

(Belonging) to Menaḥem son of	**למנחם בן**
Yishmaʿʾel	**ישמעאל**

Both these names are known in the Bible and are common on seals and among the bullae of our assemblage.

102. The right hand fragment of a bulla, containing the beginning of a two-line inscription as above, divided by a double line. This seal is slightly larger than the previous one:

(Belonging) to Menaḥem son of	**למנ[חם בן]**
Yishmaʿʾel	**ישׁ[מעאל]**

101

102

103. Menaḥem son of *Mnš*

This bulla is damaged on the bottom edge, but the inscription is intact. The linear frame encloses a two-line inscription divided by a double line:

(Belonging) to Menaḥem למנחם ב
son of Mnš ן מנש

The name *Menaḥem* is common. The second name, *Mnš*, is enigmatic and difficult to interpret. Apparently a *he* — which would yield the name Manasseh — is missing, but the space following the *shin* is smooth and nothing had been engraved there. Could this be an unusual, shortened form of the name Manasseh? A similar name, *mnṯ*, is found in Ugaritic, but its meaning is unknown.[96]

103

104. Menaḥem (son of) Pagi

This bulla is almost complete. It has a double frame and the field is divided into three registers by single lines. In the upper register is a depiction of a fish, a motif quite common on Hebrew seals (see also bulla No. 97). In the two other registers is a two-line inscription:

(Belonging) to Menaḥem למנחם
(son of) Pagi פגי

The name *Menaḥem* is common; see also above. The name in the second line is apparently to be read as *Pagi*, though the *gimel* leans somewhat to the left instead of to the right. The *pe* can be distinguished from the *gimel* by the bend at the bottom. The name Pagi apears neither in the Bible nor on seals. It is apparently derived from *pg*, "unripe fruit", as found in Song of Songs 2: 13 (the word is mistranslated as "fig" in the English versions). Compare the placename *byt pgy* (Bethphage), near Jerusalem, from the period of the Second Commonwealth. The name also appears in the Arad Inscriptions (72: 2); the similarity of *pe* and *gimel* there led Aharoni to read *ppy*, interpreting it as an Egyptian name.

104

105. Maʿaśeyahu (son of) ʾAshyahu

There are two identical bullae. The two-line inscription is divided by a row of pellets. Bulla No. 105a is complete, but finger pressure has damaged several of the

96 Gröndahl, p. 84.

letters; bulla No. 105b is broken on two sides but the inscription is better preserved:

(Belonging) to Maʿaśeyahu	**a: למעשי[הו]**	**b: [ל]מעשי[הו]**
(son of) ʾAshyahu	**אשיה[ו]**	**אשיהו**

105a

105b

The name *Maʿaśeyahu* is common in the later books of the Bible and is also found on seals (see also the next bulla). In both those bullae the two final letters, *he* and *waw*, in the first name are not visible, and there is no room for them. Thus, this might actually be a shortened name, Maʿaśi, parallel to the name ʿAśi, from the name ʿAśayahu, found on a seal. For the name *ʾAshyahu*, see above, bulla No. 33.

106

106. Mispar son of . . .

This bulla is broken on the lower left. The two-line inscription is divided by two parallel lines:

(Belonging) to Mispar son of	**למספר בן**
. . . Ywʿ. . .	**...יוע...**

The crude, clumsy script is difficult to decipher, and most of the letters are damaged. The proposed reading is not certain except, possibly, for the name *Mispar*. This name is mentioned in the Bible as one of those returning from Exile under Zerubbabel (Ezra 2: 2). The word *bn* is apparently complete, but the head of the *bet* is open at the bottom, and the proposed *nun* is of an unusual form for this period.

107. Maʿaśeyahu (son of) Ḥilqiyahu

This bulla is damaged on the right and above. The linear frame encloses a two-line inscription divided by a double line:

(Belonging) to Maʿaśeyahu — למעשי[הו]
(son of) Ḥilqiyahu — חלקיהו

The last two letters of the first line are hidden in shade in the photograph, and it subsequently proved impossible to reexamine the bulla. In contrast to the previous bulla, however, there is sufficient space for the two letters as restored to yield the name Maʿaśeyahu. For the name *Ḥilqiyahu*, see bulla No. 58. Note the somewhat distorted shape of the *qoph*.

107

108. Mṣr son of Shallum

This bulla, damaged on the upper left, bears a two-line inscription. divided by two parallel lines:

(Belonging to) Mṣr — מצר [ב]
son of Shallum — ן שלם

The script is careless. The possessive prefix *lamed* is lacking in the first line. The first name, Mṣr, is unknown, but it should perhaps be vocalized Meṣer. The angular form of the *mem* in the lower line is not common. The form of the *shin* is also unusual. For the name *Shallum*, see bulla No. 158.

108

109. Miqnemelekh....

The lower part of this bulla below the dividing lines, is lost:

(Belonging) to Miqnemelekh — למקנמלך
..... — .....

The name *Miqnemelekh* appears here for the first time on a Hebrew seal. It is known on an Ammonite seal: *ltmkʾ bn mqnmlk*.[97] This name is parallel to the Biblical name Miqneyahu. See also below, bulla No. 154.

109

110. Meshullam (son of) ʾAshyahu

This bulla is complete. The two-line inscription is divided by two parallel lines:

97 Vattioni 1978, No. 318.

110

(Belonging) to Meshullam · **למשלם ·**
(son of) ʾAshyahu **אשיהו**

The name *Meshullam* is common in the Bible, mainly in the later books, and is found on seals and on several other bullae. After the name there is a division dot. For the name *ʾAshyahu*, which appears on several bullae, see above, bulla No. 33.

111. Meshullam son of Rephaʾyahu

This bulla is broken at the top. The two-line inscription is divided by two parallel lines:

111

(Belonging) to Meshullam **לׄמׄשׄלׄםׄ בׄ**
son of Rephaʾyahu **ןׄ רפאיהו**

All the letters in the first line are decapitated. The proposed reading is not certain, and the name might read *lmšʿn*. The name *Rephaʾyahu* parallels the name Raphael; and note the shorter form Raphaʾ, appearing on bullae Nos. 42 and 141. It is also found on an unpublished seal: *lrpʾyhw bn smk*, and on a bulla from the City of David.[98]

112. Mishʿan son of Shaḥar

This complete bulla bears a two-line inscription divided by two parallel lines. At the end of the second line there are three pellets serving as space fillers:

112

(Belonging) to Mishʿan son of **למשען ב[ן]**
Shaḥar **שחר ∴**

The *nun* at the end of the first line is not visible. The name *Mishʿan* is new to us. It follows the construction of the biblical names, *Mibṣar, Mibsam* and *Mispar* (see bulla No. 105), etc. This is probably a shortened form of an unknown theophoric name, such as *Mishʿaniyahu, which expresses a desire for divine support of the new-born infant, following the passage: "The Lord was my support (*mishʿani*)" (2 Samuel 22: 19; Psalms 18: 19). Compare the names Semakhyahu and Mibtaḥyahu in the Lachish Letters, and Mibṭaḥ < Mibṭaḥyah in the Elephantine Papyri. The name *Shaḥar*, found on several bullae (Nos. 22–26), is the abbreviated form of the theophoric name Sheḥariah (1 Chronicles 8: 26).

98 Shiloh 1985, p. 80: 17.

113. Mattan son of ʾAdoniḥai son of Shaḥar

This bulla is broken on the right and below. The clay is fired brown with a black core. The three-line inscription is divided by two double lines into three registers:

(Belonging) to Mattan son of למתן בן
ʾAdoniḥai [א]דניחי
son of Shaḥar [בן ש]חר

113

The script is fine, though some of te letters are damaged or blurred. In the first name, the first letter could be either *mem* or *nun*, while the second letter is either a *taw* or a *shin*. The proposed reading, *Mattan*, seems the most reasonable. This name is common among the bullae of our assemblage. In the second name, the *aleph* is broken, but the traces seem to be of the lower part of the main stroke; the *ḥet* blends with the preceding *yod*. The name *ʾAdoniḥai* is new; similar names are ʾAbiḥai, appearing in the Arad Inscriptions (39: 11) and on Ammonite seals,[99] and ʾAsherḥai, found among the bullae of our assemblage (bulla No. 126). For the component *ḥy* in theophoric names, see the discussion under bulla No. 126.

The grandfather's name has been reconstructed as [*š*]*ḥr*, a common name among the bullae. Another possible reconstruction, [*pš*]*ḥr*, would leave insufficient room for the word *bn* (see the drawing). This is the fifth bulla recording three generations.

114–116. Mattan son of Pelaṭyahu

This person possessed three seals, two of which were almost identical. Of two seals there is a single bulla each, while of the third seal there are two bullae; this latter seal bore an architectural-floral motif.

114

114. This complete bulla has a linear frame enclosing a two line inscription divided by two parallel lines:

(Belonging) to Mattan son of למתן בן
Pelaṭyahu פלטיהו

99 Diringer, No. 103; P. Bordreuil: *Syria* 50 (1973), p. 186.

In the upper line, the third letter is damaged, while the first letter in the lower line is almost entirely obliterated. *Mattan* is the shortened form of the name Mattanyahu (see bulla No. 119). It is found in the Bible, on seals and among our bullae. For the name *Pelaṭyahu*, see above, bulla No. 86.

115. This bulla is almost entirely identical to bulla No. 114, but it has a double dividing line and the script is somewhat more elegant:

115

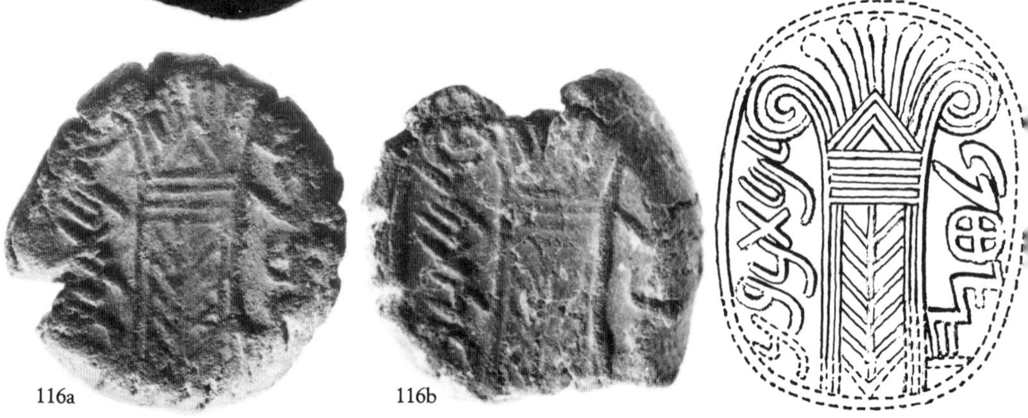

116a 116b

(Belonging) to Mattan son of Pelaṭyahu — **למתן בן**
[פ]לטיהו

116. There are two impressions of this third seal of Mattan. One of the bullae is complete while the other is slightly broken below. At the centre of the impression is a pillar supporting a "proto-Aeolic" capital of the Phoenician palmette type.[100] The trunk of the pillar is decorated with a herringbone pattern. This is a new motif on seals (compare bullae Nos. 137 and 206). The inscription is in two vertical lines, flanking the pillar:

(Belonging) to Mattan son of Pelaṭyahu — **a: למתן ב[ן]**
פלטיה[ו] — **b: למתן ב[ן]**
[פ]לטי[הו]

100 Y. Shiloh: *The Proto-Aeolic Capital and Israelite Masonry* (*Qedem* 11), Jerusalem 1979, pp. 26–49.

The letters are exceptionally large. The forms of *mem* and *nun* resemble the Moabite script in their large heads. The script in the second line is not preserved in its entirety. From the traces, a peculiar ligature of *yod* and *he* seems to appear at the end of the second line (see drawing).

117. Mattan son of Hoduyahu

117

This complete bulla has a linear frame enclosing a two-line inscription divided by a double line:

(Belonging) to Mattan son of Hoduyahu	למתן בן הודויהו

The script is fine. For the name *Mattan*, see above. For the name *Hoduyahu*, see the discussion above, bulla No. 55.

118. Mattan son of Yehozeraḥ

118

This small bulla is complete; its two-line inscription is divided by two parallel lines. Two letters have been damaged by finger pressure on the soft clay:

(Belonging) to Mattan son of Yehozeraḥ	למתן ב[ן] יהוזרח

Noteworthy among the letters is the *resh*, with its tall triangular head. Note also the lapidary form of the *zayin*. For the name *Mattan*, see above. The name *Yehozeraḥ* appears on an official's bulla from the time of Hezekiah.[101] In the Bible it appears in a different form: Zerahiah (1 Chronicles 6: 6 [MT 5: 32], etc.). Note also the hypocoristic form Zeraḥ, on bulla No. 62.

119. Mattanyahu son of Semakhyahu

119

This complete bulla has a linear frame enclosing a two-line inscription divided by a double line:

(Belonging) to Mattanyahu son of Semakhyahu	למתניהו ב ן סמכיהו

The script is fine. The *taw* in the first line is blurred. The name *Mattanyahu* is the full form of the name Mattan, common on the bullae of our

101 Hestrin-Dayagi, No. 4.

120

assemblage. It also appears in the Lachish Letters (1: 5). Semakhyahu appears once in the Bible (1 Chronicles: 26: 7), as well as on seals and in the Lachish Letters (4: 6; 11: 5).

120. Negbi son of Malkiyahu

This bulla is complete, measuring 18×14 mm. The clay is fired grey-black. The two-line inscription is divided by two parallel lines:

(Belonging) to Negbi	**לנגבי ב**
son of Malkiyahu	**ן מלכיהו**

The script is blurred, but the reading is certain. The name *Negbi* is new. This ethnicon is derived from the name of the Land of the Negeb. The personal name Negeb is found on seal-impressions on jar-handles from Beth-Shemesh and Gibeon.[102] The name *Malkiyahu* appears on two other bullae of our assemblage.

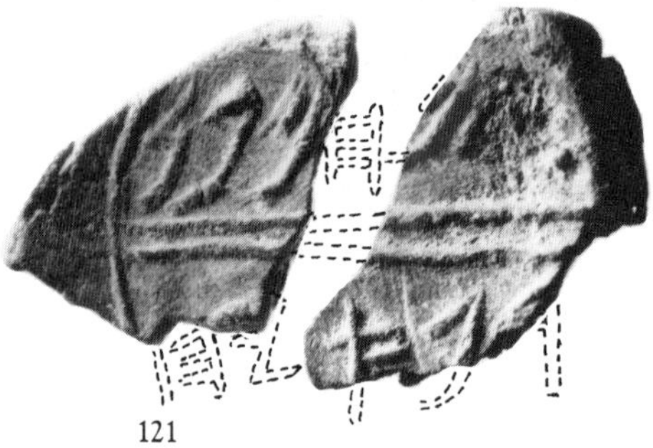

121

121. Naḥum son of Repha'yahu

Two fragments, non-contiguous, form a large bulla. Remains of a linear frame are seen, enclosing a two-line inscription divided by two horizontal lines. The letters are unusually large:

(Belonging) to Naḥum son of	**לנ[ח]ם בן**
Repha'yahu	**רפא[יהו]**

The restoration of the name *Naḥum*, with a *ḥet* in the lacuna, seems certain. The name *Repha'yahu*, though truncated, is restored in accord with the traces (part of the head of the *resh, pe* and *aleph* on the right-hand fragment, and the upper stroke of the *yod* on the other fragment) and on the basis of the complete name on bulla No. 111.

122. *Nmš* son of Neriyahu

This bulla is damaged below. It bears a two-line inscription divided by two parallel lines. The first line of script is complete, while the second line is badly damaged:

102 Moscati, p. 75: 7.

(Belonging) to N*m*š son of Neriyahu — **לנמש ב [ן] נריהו**

122

The name N*m*š appears on a Samaria Ostracon (56: 2)[103] and is apparently incised on a store-jar from Tel ʿAmal.[104] In Ugaritic there is a name *bn nmš*,[105] parallelled in Akkadian by *numušu*.[106] The meaning of this name is unknown. In the Bible the name Nimshi appears as that of the grandfather of King Jehu, "the son of Jehoshaphat the son of Nimshi" (2 Kings 9: 2, 14). Noth interpreted the latter name on the basis of the Arabic word *nims*, meaning "ferret".[107] The name *Neriyahu* is found in the Bible and is common on seals as well as among the bullae of our assemblage; see bulla No. 126.

123. N*mš*r son of Shuʿal

This complete impression has a double frame enclosing a two-line inscription divided by a compound design of two upper and lower curved lines, with a straight line between, terminating in a device resembling the Egyptian *ankh* symbol at either end, and a boss at the centre. At the end of each line of script there is a dot:

(Belonging) to N*mš*r — **לנמשר ·**
son of Shuʿal — **בן שעל ·**

123

The script is fine. The name N*mš*r is new and difficult to interpret; it is also found on the next bulla, which belongs to a different person. For the name *Shuʿal*, see above, bulla No. 69.

124. N*mš*r son of Shebanyahu

This bulla is slightly damaged, but the two-line inscription is complete. A linear frame encloses the

124

103 Diringer, p. 35. The name is generally restored as *nmš* [y], on the basis of the biblical name Nimshi, but it would now seem that such a restoration is not absolutely necessary.
104 A. Lemaire: *Revue biblique* 80 (1973), p. 557.
105 Gröndahl, pp. 28, 167.
106 Tallqvist, pp. 167, 297.
107 Noth, p. 230

inscription, which is divided by two parallel lines, on which there are three dots:

(Belonging) to N*mšr* son of **לנמשר בן**
Shebanyahu **שבניהו**

For the name *Nmšr*, see above. The name *Shebanyahu* appears on three other bullae of our assemblage.

125. Neriyahu (son of) ᵓAdoniyahu

This complete bulla is 17 mm long. A groove around the seal impression indicates that the seal-stone had been set in a metal bezel. The bulla is divided into three registers by two double lines. In the upper register there is the figure of a quadruped; its body is obliterated and only the legs are clearly visible. The other two registers contain a two-line inscription:

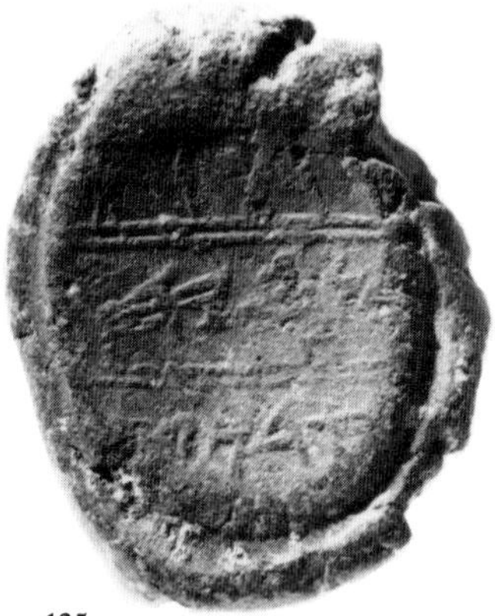

125

(Belonging) to Neriyahu **לנריהו**
(son of) ᵓAdoniyahu **אדני[הו]**

The Script is fine but slightly blurred. For the name *Neriyahu*, see the next bulla. The name *ᵓAdoniyahu* is common among the bullae of our assemblage (see bulla No. 1).

126. Neriyahu (son of) ᵓAsherḥai

Fourteen bullae were found impressed by this seal, most of them complete and some fragmentary. The impression of the seal measures 13×10 mm. There is a linear frame enclosing a two-line inscription divided by two parallel lines. Above each line of script there are three pellets, which are difficult to explain. Such pellets appear on other bullae; they are not always intended merely as space-fillers. The same phenomenon is known on Hebrew seals.

(Belonging) to Neriyahu **לנריהו**
(son of) ᵓAsherḥai **אשרחי**

The script is large and more angular than usual, though very clear. The *nun* is drawn out emphatically to the left, and the tip of its base reaches the *yod*.

The name *Neriyahu* is mentioned in the Bible only as that of the father of Baruch the scribe and of Seraiah. In contrast, it is very common on seals and among our bullae (see especially bulla No. 9, of Berekyahu son of Neriyahu). It also appears in

126a

126b

126c

126d

126e

126f

126g

126h

126i

126j

126k

126l

126m

126n

the Lachish Letters (1: 5), in the Arad Inscriptions (31: 4) and on a pottery vessel from Beersheba.[108]

The name *ʾAsherḥai* is new; it seems to combine two elements: ʾasher and ḥai. The first component is known from the Bible as the name of one of the sons of Jacob, and hence of one of the Twelve Tribes of Israel. Many commentators have considered the name in relation to the divine name Asherah, as the masculine version of this goddess.[109] It should be noted that another tribe was denoted by a foreign name — Gad, a god of fortune, traditionally considered to be the brother of Asher, both stemming from Zilpah, Leah's handmaiden. The meanings of the two names may also be related, Gad meaning "fortune" and Asher "happiness". The second component, *ḥai*, is found in such theophoric names as ʾAbiḥai,[110] Yehoḥai,[111]Yeḥiʾel, Kemoshyeḥi[112] and ʾAdoniḥai (bulla No. 113). Thus, the name ʾAsherḥai could be regarded as a theophoric name of this type, a remnant of a forgotten divinity. Compare also the name ʾAsheryaḥat on the next bulla.

The above interpretation appears to find confirmation in another biblical name: ʾAśarʾel (1 Chronicles 4: 16). Some scholars believe that the component *ʾšr* in this name was basically the name of the god ʾAsher, and interpret it as meaning "ʾAsher is ʾEl", similar to Joel, Kemoshʾel and the like. Many other scholars have contested this interpretation.[113] The name on our seal may now provide support for the above hypothesis.

127. Neriyahu (son of) ʾAsheryaḥat

127

This bulla is broken on the lower right. It is 14 mm long and the clay is fired black. The two-line inscription is divided by a ladder pattern:

(Belonging) to Neriyahu	**לנריהו**
(son of) ʾAsheryaḥat	**[א]שריחת**

The script is clear, except for the first letter in the second line, which is missing. Noteworthy among the letters is the tall *he*, the upper stroke of which extends more than usual to the right beyond the upright stroke. Similarly, the left stroke of the *shin* extends downward. The *ḥet* with two horizontal bars seems to be the only examle of this type among our bullae.

For the name *Neriyahu*, see the previous bulla. The second name, *ʾAsheryaḥat* is comprised of two elements: *ʾasher* and *yaḥat*. The restoration of the

108 Y. Aharoni (ed.): *Beer-Sheba* I, Tel Aviv 1973, p. 73.
109 *Enṣ. Miqr.* I, col. 785 (Hebrew).
110 Diringer, No. 103.
111 Aharoni, *op. cit.* (above, n. 1), p. 20.
112 Vattioni 1969, No. 111.
113 *Enṣ. Miqr.* I, col. 790 (Hebrew).

first element with an *aleph* appears to be the only possibility. Thus, this is another rare name containing the element ʾAsher (see also ʾAsherḥai on the previous bulla). The second element is common in the Bible as the personal name Yaḥat (1 Chronicles 4: 2; 6: 5, etc.). Concerning this name, S. Loewenstamm writes: "The meaning of the name Yaḥat is unknown and by way of supposition it is possible to explain this name as a shortened theophoric name from the root *ḥtt* (to break, to frighten), expressing the desire for divine wrath against the infant's enemies." [114] Compare also the name Ḥatat (1 Chronicles 4: 13), meaning "to instill fear". Indeed, our bulla would support the assumption that Yaḥat is a hypocoristic form of a theophoric name and, *ex post facto*, it supports the assumption that the element ʾAsher on the previous bulla is indeed a theophoric element. Nonetheless, the names ʾAsherḥai and ʾAsheryaḥat seem still to call for further enquiry.

128. Neriyahu son of Hiṣṣilyahu

128

The edges of this complete bulla are compressed. The two-line inscription is divided by a double line:

(Belonging) to Neriyahu — לנריהו ב
son of Hiṣṣilyahu — ן הצליהו

The script is fine. For the name *Neriyahu*, see bulla No. 126. For the name *Hiṣṣilyahu*, see above, bulla No. 49.

129. Natan (son of) ʾAḥimelek

129

This complete bulla measures 15×18 mm. The clay is fired black. The impression is divided by two double lines into three registers. The upper register contains a Phoenician palmette motif, common on Hebrew seals (see, e.g., bulla No. 6). The inscription occupies the two lower registers:

(Belonging) to Natan (son of) ʾAhi- — לנתן אח
melekh — מלך

The name *ʾAḥimelekh* is split between the two lines of script. Both names, *Natan* and ʾAḥimelekh, are known in the Bible and are common on seals. The name ʾAḥimelekh is especially common on seals, though this is its only occurrence among the bullae of our assemblage.

114 *Enṣ. Miqr.* III, col. 672 (Hebrew).

130

130. Natan (son of) Pedayahu

This complete bulla measures 15×12 mm. The clay is fired black. It has a linear frame enclosing a two-line inscription divided by a triple line:

(Belonging) to Natan	**לנתן**
(son of) Pedayahu	**פדיהו**

The name *Natan* also appears on the previous bulla. For the name *Pedayahu*, see bulla No. 99, above. Note the tall *dalet* in the latter name, the upper stroke of which continues far to the right.

131

131. *Sʾl* son of Yasaph

This complete bulla is slightly damaged on its edges. The two-line inscription is divided by two parallel lines:

(Belonging) to *Sʾl*	**לסאל ב**
son of Yasaph	**ן יסף**

The letters are large and clear. The letter *samekh* has a very distinct cursive appendix. The name *Sʾl* is new and its etymology is unknown. The name *Yasaph* is also new. This is an abbreviation of the biblical theophoric name ʾEliasaph (Numbers 1: 14, etc.), meaning "the Lord has added (a son to the family)"; alternatively it may derive from a future form, Josiphiah (Ezra 8: 10). Compare also *bʿlysp*, on a Phoenician bulla.[115]

132. Salluʾ son of Kislaʾ

This bulla is damaged around the edges. It is divided by two pairs of parallel lines into three registers. The upper register contains a depiction of a fish facing right; compare the fish on bullae Nos. 98 and 104. In the two lower registers there is a two-line inscription:

(Belonging) to *Slʾ*	**[ל]סלא ב**
son of *Kslʾ*	**ן כסלא**

The letters are large, bold and angular, and fill the entire space. The name *Slʾ*, applied to several persons, appears in the Bible in a variety of spellings:

132

115 Avigad 1964, p. 194.

Sallu — (סַלָּא), a Benjamite and head of a family who volunteered to settle in Jerusalem late in Nehemiah's time (Nehemiah 12: 7).
Sallu — (סַלּוּ), a priest who came from Babylon with Zerubbabel (Nehemiah 12: 7).
Sallu — (סָלוּא), a Simonite, father of Zimri (Numbers 25: 14).
Silla — (סִלָּא), a place near Millo (2 Kings 12: 20).

A similar spelling to that on our bulla appears on a seal inscribed *slʾ bn ʾlʾ*,[116] while on another seal[117] and on a bulla from the City of David[118] the name is spelled with the vowel letter *yod*: *sylʾ*.

The name *Kslʾ* is new, though it appears on an unpublished seal, where the final *aleph* is fully preserved. It is apparently to be interpreted as deriving from כִּסְלָה, כֶּסֶל, with the meaning of "hope, security". Compare: "So that they should set their hope (MT כִסְלָם) in God" (Psalms 78: 7); and: "...for the Lord will be your confidence (MT כְסִלֶךָ)" (Proverbs 3: 26). Hence, *Kslʾ* can be considered a hypocoristic form of an unknown theophoric name, **Kslyhw*, corresponding to the name Mibṭaḥyahu. Compare also the personal name Kislon (Numbers 34: 21) and the toponym Kesalon (Joshua 15: 10).

133. Saʿadyahu son of ...

The two bullae are damaged and broken. They bear a two-line inscription divided by a double line. Bulla No. 133a is partly broken above and below. The first line of the inscription is preserved almost completely, and only the final letter *waw* is blurred. The second line is entirely obliterated. Bulla No. 133b is represented only by the right half. In the first line, only the first four letters, *lsʿd*, are preserved, while in the second line there are only two letters:

(Belonging) to Saʿadyahu	a: לסעדיה[ו]	b: לסעד[יהו]
son of Z....	.....	[ב]ן ז[...]

133a

133b

116 M. Heltzer: "Inscribed Scaraboid Seals", in O. W. Muscarella (ed): *Ladders of Heaven*, Toronto 1981, pp. 290–293.
117 Diringer, p. 63: 36.
118 Shiloh 1985, p. 80.

The name *Saʿadyahu* is not mentioned in the Bible, but it does appear on a seal [119] and is known in later literature in the shorter form Saʿadyah. It is derived from the verb *sʿd*, "to spport"; compare: "thy steadfast love, O Lord, held me up (*ysʿdny*)" (Psalms 94: 18). The name may also appear in Arad Inscription 31: 4.[120]

134

134. ʿObadyahu son of Mattan

This damaged bulla is joined from two fragments. Its linear frame encloses a two-line inscription divided by two parallel lines:

(Belonging) to ʿObadyahu	לעבדיהו
son of Mattan	בּן מתן

The name *ʿObadyahu*, common in the Bible and on seals, appears only on this bulla in our assemblage. The name *Mattan* is found on several of our bullae.

135. ʿEzer (son of) Pelaṭyahu

The two bullae are complete and identical. The clay is fired brown. The impression is of a small, square seal (7×7 mm). This form is unique in the assemblage. It has a square linear frame, enclosing a two-line inscription divided by two parallel lines:

(Belonging) to ʿEzer	לעזר
(son of) Pelaṭyahu	פלטיהו

135a

135b

The name *ʿEzer*, a short form of ʿAzaryahu or ʾEliʿezer/ʾElʿazar, is quite common. For the name *Pelaṭyahu*, see above, bulla No. 99.

119 Bordreuil-Lemaire 1982, p. 26: 8.
120 *Arad Inscriptions*, pp. 57–58.

136. ʿAzaryahu son of Samakh

136

This bulla is broken on the lower left. The clay is fired dark brown. It has a two-line inscription divided by an ornamental element of two curved lines touching each other at the centre (their ends are missing):

(Belonging) to ʿAzaryahu לעזריה[ו]
son of Sa[makh](?) בן ס[מך]

The name *ʿAzaryahu* appears in small, partly blurred script. In marked contrast, the letters of the second line are large. Of the father's name, only the *samekh* remains. The restoration *Samakh* is conjectural, but the name could be *Slʾ* or *Sʾl*, for these names are found on other bullae.

137. ʿAzaryahu son of Pedayahu

137

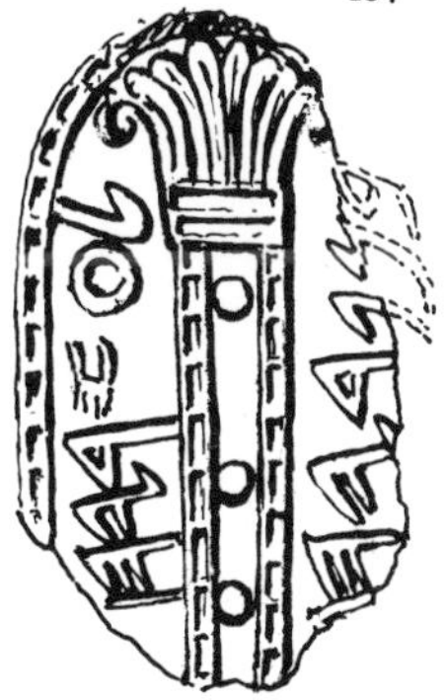

This bulla is slightly damaged on the right. The impression is a narrow, elongated oval, 17 mm long. It has a frame of ladder pattern. At the centre stands a "palmette column", ornamented with a ladder pattern along either side and three pellets running down the centre. The capital is of palmette form, with volutes flanking it. This is a new motif on Hebrew seals; compare a similar motif on bulla No. 116. The inscription flanks the column in two vertical lines:

(Belonging) to ʿAzaryahu לעזריהו
son of Pedayahu בֿןֿ פדיהו

The name *ʿAzaryahu* is common. For the name *Pedayahu*, see above, bulla No. 99. The first letters in the second line are damaged.

138. ʿAzriqam son of Parpar

Two well-preserved impressions of a single seal have been found. They measure 12×10 mm. The two-line inscription is divided by a decorative element consisting of two curved lines with a triangular device between their ends:

(Belonging) to ʿAzriqam לעזרקם
son of Parpar בן פרפר

The script is fine and clear. The name *Azriqam*, which appears also on the next bulla, is common in the Bible in various periods. One person of this name was commander of the palace in the days of Ahaz (2 Chronicles 28: 7). Another was one of the ancestors of Shemaiah, who was among those volunteering to settle in Jerusalem in the days of Nehemiah (Nehemiah 11: 15). The name means "My (divine) help has arisen" (in salvation/redemption). Compare the linguistic combinations of the elements *ʿzr* and *qm* in the Bible: *qwmh ʿzrt lnw* ("arise for our help"; Psalms 44: 27); *wqwmh bʿzrty* ("and stand up for my help"; Psalms 35: 2). Each of these elements is common in theophoric names: ʿAzaryahu, ʿAzriʾel, or ʾAḥiqam, etc. However, in the name Azriqam they are combined to form a name theophoric in nature, but without a theophoric element.

The name Parpar is also found on an Ammonite seal published recently: *lʾlyšʿ bn prpr*.[121] The editors of that seal mistakenly read the second name there as *grgr*. The *pe* on the seal is vertical in the normal Ammonite form, while on our bulla it is bent, as is usual in the Hebrew script. The reading Parpar is clear beyond all doubt. The etymology of this name is uncertain. In the Bible, it was the name of one of the two rivers in Damascus (2 Kings 5: 12). At Nuzu in Assyria, the ethnicon *parparāyu* is found as a personal name; hence there must have been a city named Parpara.[122] At Ugarit as well, *prpr* appears as a personal name.[123] The Hebrew word *pirpêr* derives from the root *prr* (to break, crumble), and has the meaning of "to move without stop, to shake, to writhe before death". In the Bible, the word appears once in the form *wayparpereni* ("he broke me asunder"; Job 16: 12), and it is more common in Mishnaic Hebrew. (The meaning of *parpar* in the sense of a butterfly was introduced into Hebrew in modern times.)

138a

138b

139. ʿAzriqam son of Ṣidqaʾ

This bulla is broken on the lower right. The double frame encloses a two-line inscription divided by a double line:

121 P. Bordreuil & A. Lemaire: *Semitica* 24 (1974), pp. 30–34.
122 C. Saporetti: *Onomastica Medio Assira* (*Studia Pohl* 6), Rome 1970, I, p. 366; II, p. 176.
123 Gröndahl, p. 174.

139

(Belonging) to ʿAzriqam **[ל]עזרקם**
son of Ṣidqaʾ **[בן] צדקא**

The script is fine. The name *ʿAzriqam* is discussed under the previous bulla. There is a close resemblance between the scripts of this name and that of the ʿAzriqam there; the two seals may have been made by the same artisan. The name *Ṣidqaʾ* is a hypocoristic form of the name Ṣidqiyahu. It is not found in the Bible, but it occurs on a Philistine seal of the 7th century BCE.[124]

140. ʿAkhbor ....

140

This bulla fragment bears the first four letters of the inscription, as well as part of the unusual ornamentation, which is difficult to explain. The double border enclosed at least one line of script:

(Belonging) to ʿAkhbor ... **לעכב[ר] ...**

The script is fine. The restoration of the surviving line is based on the name *ʿAkhbor*, meaning "mouse", found on two Hebrew seals.[125] In the Bible, Achbor the son of Micaiah is one of Josiah's ministers who was sent on the king's behalf to Huldah the prophetess (2 Kings 22: 12, 14). The patronym is entirely missing.

141. ʿAliyahu (son of) Raphaʾ

141

This complete bulla measures 14×18 mm. The impression measures 11×13 mm. The clay is fired light brown. The linear frame encloses a two-line inscription divided by two parallel lines; there are two pellets below the second line and a single one above the upper line. There is a vertical word divider at the end of the second line:

(Belonging) to ʿAliyahu **לעליהו**
(son of) Raphaʾ **רפא**

The name *ʿAliyahu* is quite rare and is not found in the Bible; see the discussion above, bulla No. 35. The letters of the name *Raphaʾ* are large and in

124 Diringer, No. 73.
125 Diringer, No. 25; Avigad 1963, p. 322.

142

higher relief, especially the *aleph*. For this name see above, bulla No. 42. Beneath the *waw* at the end of the first line, and beneath the *resh* in the second line, there are traces of letters, apparently a *bet* and a *nun* respectively. This may indicate the secondary use of an older seal, the original inscription of which has been erased.

142. ʿAliyahu (son of) Ḥeleṣ

This bulla is broken on either side. It bears a two-line inscription divided by a double line:

(Belonging) to ʿAliyahu	**לעליהו**
(son of) Heleṣ	**חלץ**

The script is blurred. The two letters in the first line are not clear, but the reading is fairly sure. For the name *ʿAliyahu*, see above. In the second line, the reading *ḥlṣ* is not absolutely certain.

143–148. Pelaṭyahu son of Hoshaʿyahu

This person possessed six seals — more than any other seal-owner represented in our assemblage of bullae. This, of course, raises questions concerning his status and function, which involved the use of so many seals and the eventual deposition of so many of his bullae within a single archive. A total of 9 bullae represents all six seals. The inscriptions on all of them are identical, with the exception of the word *bn*, which appears on only two; and one bulla is ornamented (bulla No. 147).

143a

143. Of this seal there are two impressions, one bulla complete and the other partly broken. Within the linear frame is a complete, two-line inscription divided by a double line:

(Belonging) to Pelaṭyahu	**לפלטיהו ב**
son of Hoshaʿyahu	**ן הושעיהו**

143b

The script is fine. The lines of script are slightly curved, approximately following the outline of the seal. *Pelaṭyahu*, vocalized in this way in the Bible, is one of the most common names in our assemblage of bullae; see the discussion above, bulla No. 86. The name *Hoshaʿyahu* is common in the Bible, on seals and on bullae.

144. Of this seal there are two impressions, partly broken. The inscription is as above, as are the forms of the letters and the arrangement of the lines of script. The main difference lies in the omission of the word *bn*, "son".

145. Of this third seal, the two impressions are also partly broken. The edges are missing. Between the two lines of script are two parallel dividing lines. The inscription is partly damaged. Judging from the form of the script, these three seals seem to have been made by a single artisan.

146. This bulla is damaged and blurred, and only the upper line of the inscription is completely preserved:

(Belonging) to Peḷatyahu	**לפלטיהו**
(son of) Hoshaʿyahu	**[הושע]יהו**

147. This bulla is broken on the bottom. The linear frame encloses a two-line inscription divided by a "bud design" (see bulla No. 38):

(Belonging) to Pelaṭyahu	**לפלטיהו**
(son of) Hoshaʿyahu	**הושעיהו**

The fine script would indicate that this seal, too, was made by the artisan mentioned above.

148. This is an almost complete bulla. The seal impression is smaller than the previous ones:

144 a

144b

145 a

145b

146

147

(Belonging) to Pelaṭyahu **לפלטיהו**
son of Hoshaʿyahu **בן הושעיהו**

The script here is smaller and less clear than the former. The crowding of the letters in the lower line is explained by the addition of the word *bn*. The seal seems to have been the work of a different seal-engraver from that of the above seals. Note the peculiar head of the *waw*.

148

149. Pelaṭyahu son of Ḥeleq

This complete bulla measures 15×17 mm. The clay is fired black. The linear frame encloses a two-line inscription divided by two curved lines:

(Belonging) to Pelaṭyahu **לפלטיהו**
son of Ḥeleq **בן חלק**

149

obverse

reverse

The script is small and delicate, and is difficult to read in the photograph. For the name *Pelaṭyahu*, see the previous bulla. For the name *Ḥeleq*, see bulla No. 57. It is noteworthy that another bulla, published only recently, bears the inscription: *lplṭyhw / ḥlqyhw*.[126] Ḥilqiyahu is the full form of the name Heleq.

150. *Pn*[ ] (son of) Ḥanani

This is a complete bulla. The linear frame encloses a bold two-line inscription divided by a ladder pattern. Above the upper line is a horizontal, dentated device of unclear significance:

126 Vattioni 1978, No. 379.

150

(Belonging) to *Pn*[ ] (son of) Ḥanani — לפנ[ ]ב[ ] חנני

The bold letters are in high relief and some are difficult to read. In the first line the first three letters, *lpn*, are clear, while the fourth letter is distorted. The letter *bet* following may or may not belong to the name before it, or it my be part of the word *bn*, for at the end of the line there is merely an oblique stroke which does not suit the letter *nun*. The patronym is apparently *Ḥanani*, though the form of the last letter is not sufficiently clear, and the name might be read Ḥananʾel. The name Ḥanani, a short form of Hananyahu, is known in the Bible.

151. Pashḥur son of ʾAḥiʾimoh

This bulla is complete. There are traces of a linear frame enclosing a two-line inscription divided by two parallel lines:

151

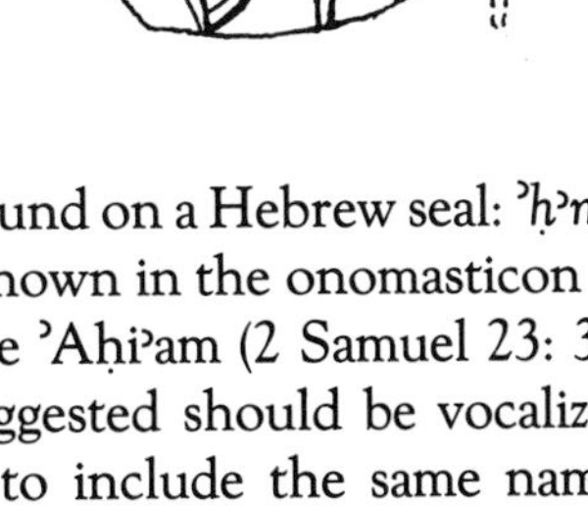

(Belonging) to Pashḥur son of ʾAḥiʾimoh — לפשחר בן אחאמה

The script is fine. The name *Pashḥur*, which appears on the next bulla as well, is an Egyptian name appearing in the Bible, borne by several persons of high rank in the period of Jeremiah (Jeremiah 20: 1–3; 21: 1; 38: 1) and by heads of priestly families in the days of Erza and Nehemiah (Ezra 10: 22; Nehemiah 10: 4). This name also appears on Hebrew seals and in the Arad Inscriptions (54). For its meaning, see the *Enc. Miqr.* V, cols. 633–635 (Hebrew).

The name *ʾḥʾmh* has two components: *ʾḥ* and *ʾm*, with the addition of the vowel letter *he* in the third person masculine, i.e. *ʾAḥi-ʾimoh*. This name is also found on a Hebrew seal: *ʾḥʾmh bn yqmyhw*.[127] Names with similar components are known in the onomasticon of the ancient Near East. In the Bible we find the name ʾAḥiʾam (2 Samuel 23: 33; 1 Chronicles 11: 35), which commentators have suggested should be vocalized *ʾAḥiʾem*. An archaic Phoenician inscription seems to include the same name: *ʾḥʾm*,[128] and in Akkadian we find the name Aḫi-um-me.[129]

127 Bordreuil-Lemaire 1976, p. 48: 8; Vattioni 1978, No. 366.
128 J. Teixidor: *BASOR* 225 (1977), pp. 70–71.
129 Tallqvist, pp. 14, 18.

152

152. Pashḥur son of Menaḥem

This complete bulla measures 15×11 mm, and is slightly damaged. The clay is fired greyish-brown. The impression shows a double frame of truncated oval or lentoid shape, measuring 8×4 mm (compare bullae Nos. 24–26). The two-line inscription is divided by an ornamental motif of "bud design" (compare above, bullae Nos. 38 and 147). At the end of the inscription is a dot:

(Belonging) to Pashḥur son of	**לפשחר בן**
Menaḥem	**· מנחם**

The script is tiny and fine. For the name *Pashḥur*, see the previous bulla. The seal of Pashḥur son of ʿAdiyahu, published by Sukenik,[130] has been ascribed to the Persian period because the priestly family of Pashḥur is mentioned in the days of Ezra and Nehemiah. Our seal, however, is pre-Exilic. The similarity in the decorative motifs on both seals is noteworthy.

153. Pataḥ son of Naḥum

This almmost complete bulla is of irregular form. A blob of clay is appended on the right, and it is broken on the left. The impression measures 9×11 mm. The double frame encloses a two-line inscription divided by a ladder pattern:

(Belonging) to Pataḥ	**לפתח ב**
son of Naḥum	**ן נחם**

153

The script is not uniform. The *taw* in the first line is distorted by scratches beside it; the *bet* at the end of this line has an open (?) head. The name *Pataḥ* is new. It is apparently a hypocoristic form of the biblical name Petaḥyah, common in the Persian period (Ezra 10: 22; Nehemiah 9: 5, etc.) and should also be associated with the name Yiphtaḥ. Compare the neo-Babylonian name Pataḫ. The name *Naḥum* can also be vocalized as Naḥam, as a short form of Nehemiah. This name is very common on seals.

154. Ṣaphan (son of) Miqneyahu

This bulla is complete. The linear frame encloses the two-line inscription which is divided by two parallel lines:

130 Moscati, Pl. XII: 4.

(Belonging) to Ṣaphan · **לצפן** ·
(son of) Miqneyahu **מקניהו**

154

The letters are large and clumsy. The first line terminates in a dot, leaving no room for the theophoric element *yhw* (see drawing). The letter *ṣade* shows a curious deformation, consisting of two parallel strokes with an upward bend of the upper stroke.

The name *Ṣaphan* is shortened from Ṣephanyahu, for which see the next bulla. The name *Miqneyahu* is found in the Bible (1 Chronicles 15: 18 — Mikneiah), on seals[131] and in the Arad Inscriptions (60: 4). On one seal a shorter form appears: *mqnyw ʿbd yhwh*.[132] See also Miqnemelekh, above, bulla No. 109. The name means "(The infant is) the property, or creation, of Yahweh".

155. Ṣephanyahu (son of) Sheʾila

This bulla is complete. The edge has been compressed on the left, but there are still traces of a double frame, enclosing a two-line inscription divided by two parallel lines:

(Belonging) to Ṣephanyahu **לצפניהו**
(son of) Sheʾila **שאלה**

155

The name *Ṣephanyahu* is common and is found in the Bible and on seals. The *ṣade* resembles a *shin* with an appended line on the right. The name *Sheʾila* is new; it is derived from the root *šʾl*, meaning "request". Some consider the name Sheʾal in the Bible (Ezra 10: 29) not as a shortened theophoric verbal name, but rather as a noun, in the meaning of *mishʾalah*, "request". We may comprehend the present in this sense as well: Sheʾila, "a supplication to God". Compare the verbal names from this same root: Sheʾaltiʾel in the Bible, and Yishʾal on a Hebrew seal.[133] The name Sheʾila is feminine in form, but it can serve as a

131 Moscati, p. 65: 44.
132 F. M. Cross: "The Seal of Miqnêyaw, Servant of Yahweh", in L. Gorelick & Elizabeth Williams-Forte (eds.), *Ancient Seals and the Bible*, Malibu 1983, pp. 55–63.
133 Vattioni 1969, No. 213.

masculine name as well; compare the biblical masculine names of feminine form: Hashubah, Hashabnah, Adnah, Jonah, etc. In the Samaria Papyri from Wadi Daliyeh, the name *yhwḥnn br šʾlh* is mentioned,[134] and on a bulla from the City of David there is the name *nḥm bn šʾlh*.[135]

156

156. *Qrbʾr* son of ʿAzarʾel

This bulla is almost complete, though its edges are worn. The linear frame encloses a two-line inscription divided by two parallel lines:

(Belonging) to *Qrbʾr*	**לקרבאר**
son of ʿAzarʾel	**בן עזראל**

The script is crude and clumsy, almost lapidary in style. The *resh* at the end of the first line, and the word *bn* in the second line, are damaged.

The rare and difficult name *Qrbʾr* appears in a full spelling, *Qrbʾwr*, in the Arad Inscriptions (24: 14).[136] Aharoni connected this name with the element *ʾur*, appearing in such names as Uri, Uriel and Uriah. The defective spelling *ʾr* on our bulla is common on seals: *ʾryhw*, *ywʾr*, etc. But the first element, *qrb*, is enigmatic, for the ordinary meanings of such a word do not lend themselves to a plausible personal name.

The name *ʿzrʾl* is unique on our bullae but common in the later books of the Bible, vocalized as *ʿAzarʾel* and, with the medial *yod*, ʿAzriʾel.

157a

157b

157. Reʾayahu (son of) Ḥeleṣyahu

Two bullae of this seal have been found. Bulla No. 157a is complete and bears a two-line inscription divided by a ladder pattern, while bulla No. 157b is the left-hand fragment of a similar bulla:

(Belonging) to Reʾayahu	**לראיהו**
(son of) Ḥeleṣyahu	**חלציהו**

The first letter in the lower line is blurred. Note the tall *yod* with triangular head, in the same line. The name *Reʾayahu* appears in the later books of the Bible, in the shorter form Reʾayah. One person

134 F. M. Cross: "Samaria Papyrus 1: An Aramaic Slave Conveyance of 335 B.C.E. Found in the Wadī ed-Daliyeh", *EI* 18 (1985), pp. 7*–17*, especially p. 8*.
135 Shiloh 1985, p. 80: 51.
136 J. Naveh has drawn my attention to the occurrence of another *Qrbʾwr*, in *Arad Inscriptions* 34: 3 (the blurred name was erroneously read *ndbyhw* by the editor).

so named was among the Netinim who returned from Exile with Zerubbabel (Ezra 2: 47; Nehemiah 7: 50). The name signifies "Yahweh saw (*r'h*) the suffering of the parents and gave them the infant". Compare "the Lord has looked upon my affliction" (Genesis 29: 32). Similar names are Yaḥzeyah and Ḥazael. For the name *Ḥeleṣyahu*, see above, bulla No. 47.

158–160. Shallum son of 'Elishamaʿ

This person possessed three similar seals, differentiated only by the size of the script and the use of the word *bn*. Of each seal there is only part of a single bulla.

158. This bulla is broken on the left and below. It has a linear frame enclosing a two-line inscription divided by two parallel lines:

(Belonging) to Shallum לשלם ב
son of 'Elishamaʿ ן אלשמ[ע]

158

The script is blurred. The word *bn* is divided. The end of the second line is missing.

The name *Šlm* is vocalized in the Bible as *Shallum*. This is a theophoric name, a shortened version of Shelemyahu, in the sense of "Yahweh has recompensed". The name is common at the end of the period of the Judean monarchy and among those who returned from Exile in the Persian period. The persons so named include the uncle of the Prophet Jeremiah, father of Hanam'el (Jeremiah 32: 7). It is found on seals and in the Elephantine Papyri. For *'Elishamaʿ* see above, bulla No. 4.

159. This bulla is broken on the right. The left portion of the inscription has survived. The inscription is as above:

(Belonging) to Shallum son of [לשל]ם בן
'Elishamaʿ [אל]שמע

159

160. This bulla fragment contains the beginnings of two lines of script. Despite the scanty traces, the inscription can be restored; the script is larger than the above:

(Belonging) to Shallum son of לשל[ם בן]
'Elishamaʿ אל[שמע]

160

161

161. Shallum son of Hosha῾yahu

This bulla is almost complete. The two-line inscription is divided by two parallel lines. There are three pellets below the second line:

(Belonging) to Shallum son of Hosha῾yahu	**לשלם ב[ן] הושעיהו**

The script is careless and blurred. For the names, see above.

162

162. Shema῾yahu (son of) Ya᾿azan

Two fragments join to form this bulla. The linear frame encloses a two-line inscription divided by a double line:

(Belonging) to Shema῾yahu (son of) Ya᾿azan	**[ל]שמעיהו יאזן**

The script is fine. The name *Shema῾yahu* is common in the Bible, on seals and among the bullae of our assemblage. The name of the father here, *Ya᾿azan*, is an otherwise unknown shortened form of the theophoric name Ya᾿azanyahu, found in the Bible and on seals. Two letters are partly damaged.

163

163. Shema῾yahu .....

This bulla is almost complete. The two-line inscription is divided by a double line. Only the upper line of script can be deciphered:

(Belonging) to Shema῾yahu	**לשמעיהו**
......	......

The inscription is very blurred. The patronym is illegible, but it seems to differ from that on the previous bulla.

164. Shu῾al son of Yishma῾᾿el

This bulla is almost complete. The two-line inscription is divided by two parallel lines:

(Belonging) to Shu῾al son of Yishma῾᾿el	**לשעל בן ישמעאל**

The script is somewhat blurred, but the reading is certain. For the name *Shuʿal*, which appears on three other bullae, see above, bulla No. 69. The name *Yishmaʿʾel* is common on our bullae. See the same two names, but in inverted order, on bulla No. 79.

164

165. Shephaṭyahu (son of) ʾAdoniyahu

This bulla is complete. The linear frame encloses a two-line inscription divided by two parallel lines terminating on either side in a simple lily motif:

(Belonging) to Shephaṭyahu לשפטי[הו]
(son of) ʾAdoniyahu ארניהו

In the first line the letters are not sufficiently clear. The reading of the first name, *Shephaṭyahu*, is most likely, though the name Shemaʿyahu would also be possible. In contrast, the name of the father, *ʾAdoniyahu*, is quite clear. For this name, see above, bulla No. 1.

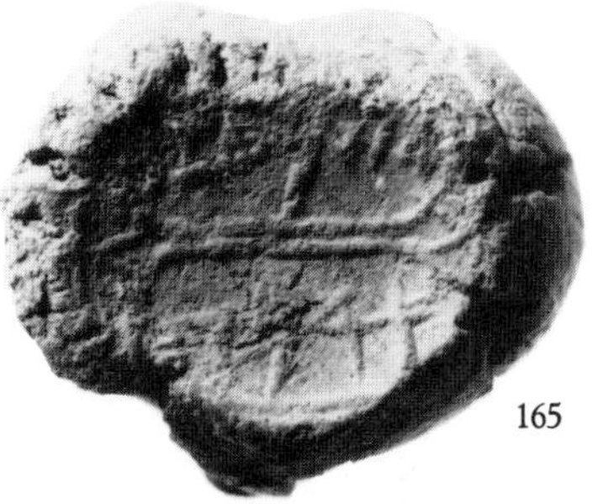

165

166. Shaphaṭ son of ʾAḥiyahu

This bulla is broken. The linear frame encloses a two-line inscription divided by two parallel lines:

(Belonging) to Shaphaṭ son of לשפט בנ[ן]
ʾAḥiyahu אֹחיהו

Above the upper line are two pellets, as on other bullae. The name *Shaphaṭ* is an abbreviated form of Shephaṭyahu and is found in the Bible and on seals. The name *ʾAḥiyahu* appears in the Bible in the shorter form ʾAḥiyah, as the name of a priest in the days of Saul, of the father of King Baasha and of a prophet. It is found on seals and in the Lachish Letters (3: 17).

166

167. Shebanyahu (son of) Śerayahu

This bulla is complete. The linear frame encloses a two-line inscription divided by two parallel lines:

167

(Belonging) to Shebanyahu לשבני[הו]
(son of) Śerayahu שריהו

The last letters in each line are blurred. For the name *Shebanyahu*, see above. For the name *Śerayahu*, see the discussion above, bulla No. 37.

168. Tanḥum (son of) Hiṣṣilyahu

168

This bulla is broken on the left. The two-line inscription is divided by two parallel lines:

(Belonging) to Tanḥum לתנח[ם]
(son of) Hiṣṣilyahu הצל[יהו]

The inscription is partly blurred and partly missing. In the first line the reconstruction *tnḥm* is certain. The name *Tanḥum* appears on impressions of several Hebrew seals, on an Ammonite seal[137] and in the Arad inscriptions (39). In the Bible the form Tanhemet appears as a masculine name. The name has a meaning similar to that of Naḥum. The second line is difficult to read because of the unusual form of the *ṣade*, and the name might simply read *hṣl*; the restoration, however, seems certain. For the meaning of the name *Hiṣṣilyahu*, see above, bulla No. 49.

Enlarged 4:1

169

C. Fragmentary Bullae Preserving the Patronymic

169. ..... son of Gaddiyahu

This bulla is broken above and on the left. The clay is fired black. It is 11 mm long. The impression is divided into three registers by two pairs of parallel lines. The upper register is broken; the middle register depicts a grazing gazelle facing left, a motif typical of Hebrew seals.[138] This register also contains the two letters *bn*, "son of". The lower register contains the patronym:

....
son of בן
Gaddiyahu גדיהו

137 Avigad 1970, p. 288: 5.
138 Avigad 1979, Pl. ב: 14.

The script is tiny and fine. The name of the seal's owner is missing. The word *bn* is unusually placed on the left of the middle register, above the head of the quadruped. In the lower register is the patronym. The name *Gaddiyahu* is common on seals, and it is found on other bullae of our assemblage.

170

170. The middle part of a bulla which had been divided into three registers. In the upper register, now missing, there was apparently the name of the owner of the seal. In the middle register there remains the patronym, דמליהו — *Demalyahu*, and the word *bn*, son of. This latter word indicates that the name of the grandfather must have been in the lower register. However, the uppr register may have contained some ornamental design; in this case the inscription would have been limited to the two lower registers, and only two generations would be represented (compare bullae Nos. 125 and 129). For the name *Demalyahu*, see bulla No. 46.

171

171. The lower fragment of a bulla, preserving the name יהוק[ם] — *Yehoqam*.

172

172. The lower part of a bulla, containing the name יקמיה[ו] — *Yeqamyahu*.

173

173. This damaged bulla bears a two-line inscription divided by a double line. The upper line of script is illegible; in the lower line the patronym has survived: ישמעאל — *Yishmaʿel*.

174. This broken bulla bears a two-line inscription divided by two parallel lines. In the upper line are traces of the letters: לשו[ע]ל ב[ן] — *(Belonging) to Shuʿal son of*; the lower line reads: מל[כ]יה[ו] — *Malkiyahu*.

174

175

176

177

175. This bulla fragment bears the patronym מלכ[יהו] — *Malkiyahu*.

176. This lower fragment of a bulla contains the lower line of the inscription: בן נחם — *son of Naḥum*.

177. This damaged bulla bears a very blurred two-line inscription. In the lower line it is just possible to read: עזיה[ו] — *ʿUzziyahu*.

178. This damaged bulla bears a two-line inscription divided by two parallel lines terminating in an indefinite ornamental pattern. In the lower line is the patronym פדיהו — *Pedayahu*.

179. This damaged bulla bears a two-line inscription divided by two parallel lines. Of the first name, only the final letters *yhw* remain; in the second line is the patronym שמעיה[ו] — *Shemaʿyahu*.

180. These are two bullae fragments preserving the patronym *Shephaṭyahu*. Bulla No. 180a preserves the letters בן שפט[יהו], whereas bulla No. 180b has [שפ]טיהו. It is not certain that both these impressions are from the same seal.

178

179

180a

180b

D. Fragmentary Bullae Preserving Incomplete Names

181. The left part of a bulla bearing a two-line inscription divided by two parallel lines. At the end of the upper line are the letters מב[; and below, the letters יאל[.

182. The left part of a bulla, bearing a two-line inscription divided by a ladder pattern. At the end of the upper line are the letters שע[; and below:]יה[.

183. The left part of a bulla bearing a two-line inscription divided by two parallel lines. In the top line are the letters ידו[; and below: חר[, possibly to be restored as [פש]חר.

184. The right fragment of a bulla bearing a two-line inscription divided by two parallel lines. The upper line reads: למ]; and below: בן.

185. The left part of a bulla bearing a two-line inscription divided by two parallel lines. In the first line there are traces of the four final letters: עידו[. This might be restored in several ways: [יש]עידו, [הוש]עידו or [שמ]עידו. Below, too, the four final letters are preserved: שידו[, which can be restored as [א]שידו or [מע]שידו.

186. The left part of a bulla bearing a two-line inscription divided by two parallel lines. Above and below are preserved the letters ידו[.

187. The left part of a bulla bearing a two-line inscription divided by an unusual strip tapering toward the centre. Above and below are traces of the letters ידו[. Note the unique form assumed by the lower *he* as a result of the horizontal stance of the

181

182

183

184

185

186

187

upper stroke, its shift to the right of the vertical stroke, and its blending in with the two lower strokes.

188

188. The left part of a bulla, bearing a linear frame enclosing a two-line inscription divided by two parallel lines. Of the inscription, only traces remain; in the upper line: ניהו[; and in the lower line: הו[.

189. The upper part of a bulla bearing the letters]ליהו.

189

190. The right part of a bulla bearing a two line inscription divided by two parallel lines. Above are the letters ליהו, and below:]עיה[.

191. The left part of a bulla bearing a linear frame enclosing a two line inscription divided by two parallel lines ending in a simple palmette motif. In the first line, the name ended איהו[, which might be restored in various ways: [רפ]איהו, [ר]איהו, [יר]איהו or [פל]איהו. The first two names in this brief list are found among the bullae of our assemblage.

190

192. The lower part of a bulla bearing four letters of the patronym ליהו[ ]. This might be restored as [א]ליהו or [הצ]ליהו. In the upper line there are traces of the letters יהו[.

191

192

193. Fragment of a bulla with a double dividing line in the middle, below which are the letters]יה[; above are traces of several letters.

194. Fragment of a bulla with a double dividing line in the middle, above which are the letters]יהו ב and below which are the letters]עי[.

195. Fragment of a bulla with a triple dividing line in the middle, above which are two letters in high relief and traces of a third letter:]עמל. This can possibly be restrored as the name ʿAmalyahu.

196. Fragment of a bulla similar in character to the previous fragment. Bearing three irregular dividing lines, above which are the letters]לשל, apparently to be restored as the name Shallum.

197. Left-hand fragment of a large bulla with a linear frame and two parallel dividing lines, above which are the letters]ליהו[, which can be restored as the name ʾEliyahu or Ḥiṣṣilyahu.

198. Left-hand fragment of a bulla with a double dividing line in the middle, with several indeterminate marks above and below.

193

194

195

196

197

198

199

200

E. Bullae Bearing Ornamental Motifs

199. A bulla bearing the figure of a two-winged scarab, symbolizing the sun, which holds a ball of dung between its forelegs. Below the scarab there is an inscription, of which only the letters]ניהו remain. This is apparently to be restored as the name ʾAdoniyahu.

200. This broken bulla bears a four-winged *uraeus* (cobra), below which there is an inscription, only one letter of which, a *resh*, can clearly be read.

201. A broken bulla bearing a four-winged *uraeus*, as above. Below the latter is the upper edge of a palmette (see the figure). This is apparently one of the well-known motifs of an Egyptian divinity (Horus, scarab, *uraeus*, etc.), seated or standing on a lotus flower.[139] Above the *uraeus* there are traces of several letters(?). The scarab and *uraeus* are Egyptian mythological motifs. Hebrew seals borrowed them from Phoenician iconography.[140]

202. Fragment of a bulla bearing the figure of a bird flanked by remains of an inscription. The bird motif appears on seals,[141] but it has not yet been found on an inscribed seal as a central motif in such

201

202

139 Avigad 1979, Pl. א: 4.
140 Avigad 1979, Pl. ב: 15.
141 Avigad 1968, Pl. 4: C.

a realistic form. To the right of the bird are traces of the two final letters of the first line: חם[. To the left are traces of the two final letters of the second line of the inscription: בע[, preceded by the left edge of the letter *shin*. Thus, we can restore the first name as *Naḥum* and the second name as *Sheba*ʿ. The Bible mentions Sheba the son of Zikri, who rebelled against David (2 Samuel 20: 1); this name also appears on a Hebrew seal[142] and on a Samaria Ostracon (2: 6).

203

203. The right part of a bulla bearing the figure of a horned quadruped facing right, above which are two letters: זין or צין.

204

204. A partly broken bulla bearing a hatched frame enclosing a quadruped, the neck of which is thin and tall, with the vestigial head (?) turned back. In front of the neck there is a row of oblique lines. This stylized animal occupies most of the area of the impression, and in the open spaces there are no letters.

205

205. A bulla broken above, in the centre of which stands the trunk of a palm-tree, with bunches of dates (?) above. There is no inscription.

206

206. The upper fragment of a bulla, bearing a proto-Aeolic capital motif of Phoenician palmette type, common in ivory carving.[143] The execution is superb. Compare bulla No. 116, above.

142 Avigad 1975, p. 69: 14.
143 Crowfoot & Crowfoot, *op. cit.* (above, n. 16), Fig. 9, Pl. 21: 1.

F. Illegible Bullae

207. Bulla bearing traces of horizontal dividing lines and of illegible letters.

208. Bulla bearing numerous groups of parallel lines, scattered over the surface.

209. Bulla on which there are traces of letters, but too vague to be read.

210. Broken bulla bearing traces of dividing lines and of illegible letters.

211. Bulla on which the entire inscription has been lost except for several traces.

207

208

209

210

211

3. PALAEOGRAPHY AND ORTHOGRAPHY

The study of ancient Hebrew seals often encounters difficulties in determining the date of seals according to criteria of script forms. Whereas with cursive script, written in ink or incised, changes gradually occur in letter forms and it is thus possible to trace their chronological development, the script appearing on seals, which is engraved into hard stone, is necessarily formal and conservative, retained by the seal-cutters for reasons of tradition and professional convenience over an extended period.

Hence, the script appearing on seals is difficult to ascribe to specific, limited periods, and it is not always possible to distinguish between the script of the 8th century and that of the 7th century BCE, especially in the absence of certain "key letters". From the palaeographic viewpoint, the great importance of the present group of bullae lies in the large number of bullae, in the variety of forms of script and, mainly, in the fact that the entire assemblage can be dated with certainty to the last quarter of the 7th century and the early 6th century BCE. Even though a lengthy palaeographic discussion of the date of the assemblage can thus be by-passed, we are still faced with the need for palaeographic analysis of the script in order to exploit the bullae to the utmost. In this field the amount of dated epigraphic material is small, and thus our assemblage represents a significant contribution toward the consolidation and advancement of research.

Fortunately, not all the seals impressed on the bullae were the standardized products of a single workshop: on the contrary, numerous hands are apparent in the carving of the seals, some of them highly skilled and others merely skilled or mediocre; and some were entirely amateurish and almost inadequate. Thus, we have before us a wide range of "handwritings", the product of numerous persons engaged in seal engraving. It is evident that the differences between these qualities of script have no chronological significance whatsoever.

In our palaeographic treatment, we have classified the script on the bullae into three typological groups. This division is preliminary and arbitrary, and does not presume to be precise or absolute. There is probably much overlapping between the groups, and the object of this exercise is merely to demonstrate graphically, in general terms, what has been stated above.

1. Classical Hebrew script, as exemplified in Judah by the style of the script of the Siloam Inscription (700 BCE): this is a formal, semi-cursive, pleasing script which adheres to the rules of calligraphic writing. It was a sort of Judean chancellery script. Some of its distinguishing features are as follows: the *aleph* has two parallel strokes above. The *bet* has a horizontal base and triangular head. The horizontal strokes of the *he* often tend to converge, sometimes even meeting at the left. The upper stroke often extends to the right, beyond the vertical stroke. The *ḥet* has three horizontal strokes. The horizontal strokes of the *yod* also occasionally tend to

Group 1

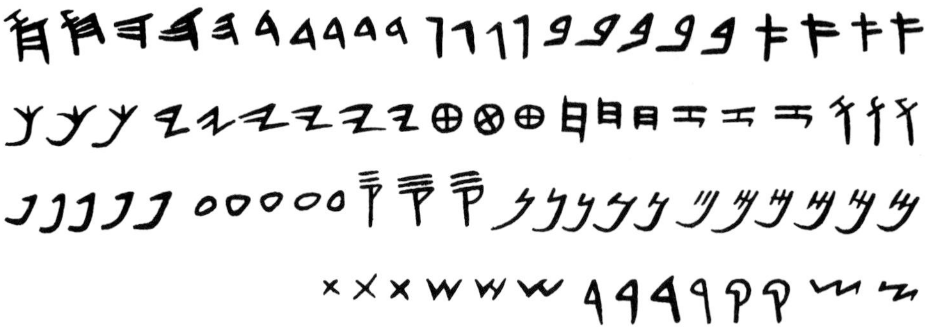

Group 2

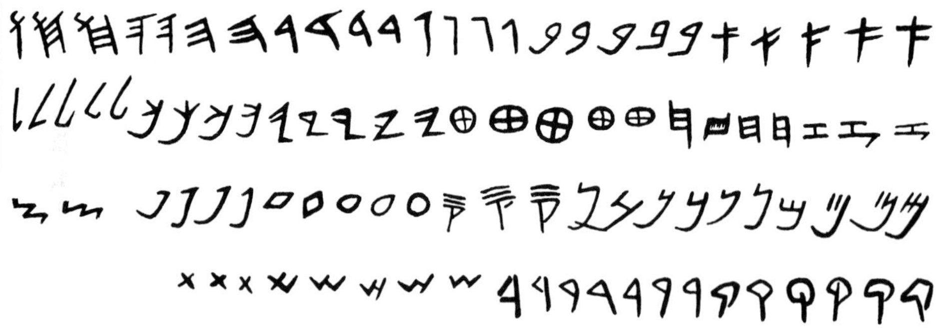

Group 3

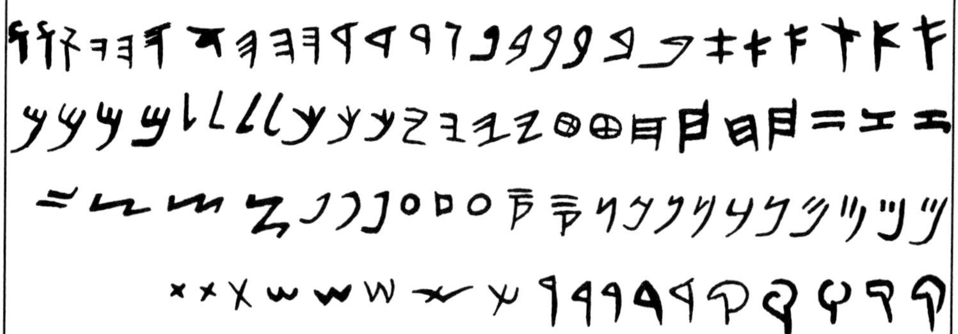

Table of scripts on the bullae

converge at the left. The *lamed* has a rounded or flattened base. The *ṣade* is cursive, in zigzag form. The head of the *qoph* is in the form of three-quarters of a circle. The *taw* is of X form. In this palaeographic group we have included such bullae as Nos. 1–5, 7–8, 11, 24, 31, 33, 50, 63–64, 66, 69, 70, 72, 90, 123, 128 and 143.

2. This script is similar in principle to the previous group, but is less strictly uniform in letter shapes and in its 'calligraphy'. The group encompasses a majority of the bullae, good examples of which are Nos. 6, 9, 20, 35, 53–55, 57–58, 68, 75, 98, 104, 126, 129, 131–132, 138, 141, 145, 155 and 157.

3. This script is cruder, careless and sometimes vulgar: the basic elements of the two previous groups of script are generally retained, but carelessness and lack of knowledge have led to deviant letter forms. Thus, for instance: the *aleph* on Nos. 15 and 65; the *he* on Nos. 41 and 187; the *mem* on Nos. 15, 16, 46, 108 and 154; the *ṣade* on Nos. 154 and 168; the *shin* on Nos. 34 and 108. Compare also Nos. 18, 29, 73, 81, 95–97, 105, 107, 116, 121, 150, 153 and 161. Note, however, that distorted letter forms occasionally also resulted from faulty impression into the soft clay.

As regards the orthography of the bullae, there is a tendency toward defective spellings, though this is not consistent; for example: defective — *ʿr* (at Lachish and Arad: *ʿyr*); *spr* (as on the seals); *šʿl* (as on the seals; in the Bible: *šwʿl*); *yʾs* (at Lachish: *yʾws*); *qrbʾr* (at Arad: *qrbʾwr*); full spellings — *myr[b]* (in the Bible: *mrb*); mixed spellings — *ʾlsmk* and *ʾlysmk*; *ʾlʿz* and *ʾlyʿz*; omissions of letters — on No. 3, the definite article *he* was omitted inadvertently before the word *byt*, which should have read *hbyt*.

4. THE NAMES

The onomasticon of our assemblage of bullae contains 132 different (as opposed to repeated and duplicate) names. The variety of the names was originally even greater, but many have been lost or partly lost through damage to the bullae. Naturally, these names more or less reflect those appearing on Hebrew seals in general. About two-thirds of the names find mention in the Hebrew Bible, while the remaining third are mostly known from seals and sealings, or from other epigraphic sources. There are, however, numerous innovations, such as unknown variants of biblical names: *gʿly* (biblical *gʿl*); *yʾzn* (biblical *yʾznyhw*); *yhwʾḥ* (biblical *ʾḥyhw*); *ysp* (biblical *ywspyh*); *nmš* (biblical *nmšy*); *ptḥ* (biblical *ptḥyh*); *šʾlh* (biblical *šʾl*), and so forth. Especially noteworthy is a group of new, unusual names, such as *ʾdnyḥy*, *ʾšrḥy*, [*ʾ*]*šryḥt*, *kslʾ*, *mnš*, *mṣr*, *mšmš*, *nmšr*, *sʾl*, *prpr*, and so forth. The most common names in the assemblage are Neriyahu (9 times), Yishmaʿʾel (9), Hoshaʿyahu (7), Mikhayahu (7), Pedayahu (6) and Menaḥem (5).

We should note that of all 255 bullae there is not even one belonging to a woman. As Israelite women are known to have possessed seals of their own (about a dozen have been noted to date), it might be expected that at least one bulla giving the name of a woman would be included in such a large assemblage, but this is not the case.

Each inscription contains a standardized formula giving the name of the seal owner and his patronymic. The word *ben*, "son (of)", is often omitted — not always through lack of space. On five bullae (Nos. 21, 23, 63 [incomplete], 79 and 113), the name of the grandfather is also given. Often a patronymic is shared by two, three or four seal-owners, but it is impossible to determine whether any of these instances reflect common parentage. There is not even a single instance of the personal name of the seal-owner appearing alone, without a patronymic or a title. On Hebrew seals in general, however, many such examples are known.

Most of the names are theophoric — whether in full form or hypocoristic — and they generally include the Yahwistic divine name. As was common in Judah in this period, the theophoric names begin or end with the divine element *yhw* (some 80 names in our assemblage). The shorter form *yw*, common in the northern Kingdom of Israel (as in the Samaria Ostraca) and, to a certain extent, in Judah down to the 8th century BCE, is entirely absent from our onomasticon. The suffix *yh* also seems to be entirely lacking. There are, however, names in which it is difficult to discern the final *waw* of the component *yhw*; it was omitted through lack of space, or it blended into the line of the frame, or that particular spot on the bulla is blurred. The fact that there is no clear instance of a name ending in *yh* is noteworthy, in light of the fact that many of the names on the bullae are especially common in the later books of the Bible, where the *yh* suffix frequently appears in theophoric names.[144] In the Lachish Letters and the Arad Inscriptions, too, the *yhw* ending is exclusively employed.

144 Z. Zevit: "A Chapter in the History of Israelite Personal Names", *BASOR* 250 (1983), pp. 1–16.

The divine element *ʾel* appears in only eight of our names, and names with the archaic theophoric elements *ʾab* and *ʾaḥ* are very few.

Among the "secular" names in the assemblage, there are several which also appear in the Bible and derive from names of animals: Hagab, "grasshopper", ʿAkhbor, "mouse", Shuʿal, "fox". Other names derive from geographical features, such as Karmi, Negbi.

We may also note an entire lack of "foreign" names, with the exception of the name Pashhur, which, though of Egyptian origin, was early adopted into the Hebrew onomasticon.

5. ICONOGRAPHY

Most inscribed West Semitic seals also bear some kind of figurative motif. Hebrew seals, though of this general cultural horizon, are ornamented to a much lesser extent; this is clearly demonstrated by our bullae, the bulk of which bear little more than their inscriptions.

Hebrew seals drew their decorative motifs mostly from Phoenician art, which overwhelmingly utilized Egyptianizing themes. Two main figurative motifs adopted on Hebrew seals are the scarab (bulla No. 199) and the *uraeus* (cobra, bullae Nos. 200–201), both originally Egyptian mythological creatures. Such motifs also underwent certain graphic changes: the two-winged scarab of Egypt was often depicted as four-winged, and the two-winged *uraeus* of Egypt was frequently rendered on Hebrew seals with four wings (as on our bullae).

In contrast, Mesopotamian influence is rather sparse on Hebrew seals. In this respect, the scene on bulla No. 10 is unique. The only other human figure in our assemblage appears on bulla No. 77.

In our assemblage animal motifs are more frequent, outstanding among which is the graceful gazelle on bulla No. 169. This motif seems to appear exclusively on Hebrew seals. Bulla No. 203 depicts another, unidentified quadruped, as does bulla No. 125; and the very stragne, stylized quadruped of bulla No. 204 is intriguing from the artistic point of view. Birds are represented in our assemblage by one well-executed example (bulla No. 202). Another living creature found on our bullae is the fish, rather crudely executed on three examples (bullae Nos. 98, 104 and 132). This motif is especially typical of Hebrew seals.

All in all, 13 bullae bearing decorations of this sort are included in our assemblage. Statistically, this is a very small proportion indeed, among a total of 255 bullae. It has long been maintained that Judean seals and seal-impressions of the 7th century BCE generally bore only inscriptions, without accompanying figurative representations. This phenomenon has been attributed to the religious reforms introduced by King Josiah (639–609 BCE), which seem to have involved stricter implementation of the Second Commandment forbidding graven images. This assumption, based hitherto on sporadic finds, is now strikingly confirmed by our bullae, providing a firm statistical and chronological basis for this conclusion. Further, the group of 50 bullae from the City of David excavations — contemporary with our assemblage — also lacks figurative representations, with the exception of a single bird.

Purely ornamental designs are more common. A special feature is a variety of devices appearing between the two lines of Hebrew script. Besides pairs or triplets of simple parallel lines, there are pairs of parallel lines curving outward toward their ends and terminating in floral or geometric elements (bullae Nos. 30, 31, 37, 70, 138, 165 and 191), or a horizontal design composed of a central boss with flanking "buds", which we have termed "bud design", for want of a better conventional term (bullae Nos. 38, 147 and 152). Another common ornamental motif is the

"Phoenician palmette" (bullae Nos. 6, 14, 47, 58, 75 and 129), a very frequent feature in Phoenician ornamental art. A related design, not previously encountered on seals, is the "palmette column" (bullae Nos. 116 and 137). Related to this latter motif is the "proto-Aeolic" palmette capital (bulla No. 206). Another innovation is the attractive pomegranate design on bulla No. 24. All these devices occur only on Hebrew seals.

6. CONCLUSIONS

As noted above, we know nothing of the circumstances of the discovery of the bullae, but there is no doubt that they comprise a homogeneous, uniform assemblage, found together at a single site which, apparently, had contained an archive of documents. This conclusion derives from the data discussed above, which indicate that the bullae had served to seal papyrus documents. These documents themselves appear to have been consumed in a fire, while the bullae survived.

Statistics show that in total there were 255 bullae, impressed with at least 211 different seals. Of these, 168 of the seal-owners are known to us by name, and it can be assumed that the original total of persons involved in sealing the bullae was closer to 200. The number of documents in the archive cannot accurately be estimated, for we cannot know how many bullae there were on each document; nor is it known whether all the original bullae were recovered from the site. In any event, this was certainly a rich archive, containing a large number of documents. But was it a public archive or merely a family one? This, too, cannot unequivocally be answered, though it was more likely a public archive.

The contents of the bullae and their classification according to the status of the seal-owners may perhaps be indicative of the character of the archive and of the type of documents it contained. First and foremost, we should note the fact that nine of the seal-owners represented here were senior royal Judean officials: two persons designated "who is over the house" (the highest office at the royal court, after the king); two ministers designated "servant of the king"; three "sons of the king" (apparently princes of the royal line); a "governor of the city" (most probably the minister responsible for Jerusalem, the capital); and one "scribe" (who, if in royal service, was also considered a minister). All these officials can be assumed to have used their seals in the course of their duties on official documents, that is, on administrative and legal documents. However, most of the bullae are not of officials, or in any event not of title-bearing officials. They were impressed with seals of the "private" type, bearing personal names but no titles. We have seen that some of the seal-owners possessed more than one seal, and one of them, Pelaṭyahu son of Hoshaʿyahu, even had six seals (!), all of which he used. What is surprising is that impressions of all six of these seals were found in a single archive. They may have been used to seal documents at different places, after which the documents reached this one archive. A person requiring six different seals was surely very active in his affairs. Another individual, Neriyahu son of ʾAsherḥai, used his single seal to impress fourteen bullae — that is, fourteen different documents.

Such activities may indicate that these persons were also functionaries fulfilling official duties without this fact finding expression on the bullae. There are, indeed, instances of "private" seal-impressions appearing on royal store-jars of the period of the First Temple, alongside "Lammelekh" stamps.[145] These seal-owners may well

145 D. Ussishkin: *BASOR* 223 (1976), pp. 114.

have been officials responsible for the production of the "Lammelekh" jars, for their contents or for their marketing, and they bore no specific titles. Officials of certain ranks apparently did not have defined titles, though they did fulfil various official duties calling for the use of seals. In the excavations at Arad, three seals of one ʾElyashib son of ʾAshyahu came to light. This ʾElyashib seems to have been the commander of the fortress there, for most of the letters discovered in the fortress are addressed to him; but he, too, bears no official title.[146] In this cotext we may cite an Arad ostracon in which a person named Naḥum is ordered to take oil from ʾElyashib and to seal it under his own seal (Arad Inscription 17).

On the basis of the composition of these bullae alone, we could assume that this was a royal archive of documents and letters dealing with state administration. But many of the seal-owners, possibly even the majority, seem to have been private citizens rather than officials, and some of them may even have been of the lower classes, of such limited means that they apparently prepared their own seals in order to be able to seal a document. This may be indicated by the careless execution and clumsy forms of many of the inscriptions. Thus, the archive may well have been a collection of administrative and legal documents concerning a broader public, sealed not only by officials but mainly by persons who required legal documents — sealed contracts concerning property and wealth, payment of taxes, lawsuits and the like.

So far no bullae of the First Temple period have been found still attached to their papyri; thus we have not been able to learn of the precise manner in which they were used, or of the contents of the documents thus sealed. We must therefore attempt to reconstruct the *Sitz im Leben* of these bullae by utilizing the data available to us from archaeology and from historical sources, including the Bible.

The use of papyrus scrolls, and their sealing with bullae of clay, certainly derived from Egypt, the homeland of papyrus.[147] But it must be noted that in none of the neighbouring cultures, including Egypt, has so large a hoard of bullae bearing private names come to light from the period of the Judean monarchy. In Mesopotamia in this period, cylinder-seals were generally used, though stamp-seals were already common there as well; but only a few of these stamp-seals bore names (in Aramaic). Since the latter too were impressed directly on inscribed clay tablets, there was no need for small bullae of our sort, which were thus not normally employed. In Syria and Phoenicia, only a few bullae have so far come to light. In Transjordan, too, where a relatively large number of Ammonite and Moabite seals have been found, only isolated bullae have been discovered.

While other peoples commonly used anepigraphic, iconographic seals, the Israelites preferred seals bearing their private names. This is indicative of the extent of

146 *Arad Inscriptions*, Nos. 105–107.

147 J. H. Johnson: "Private Name Seals in the Middle Kingdom", in M. G. Gibson & R. D. Biggs (eds.): *Seals and Sealings in the Ancient Near East* (*Bibliotheca Mesopotamica* 6), Malibu 1977, pp. 141–145; and see also p. 151.

literacy amongst broad sections of the Israelite population, particularly in the 7th century BCE. However, it should be noted that the excavations at Samaria, capital of the northern Kingdom of Israel, yielded a large group of bullae. Most of them crumbled to dust, but the fifteen preserved examples bore no script whatsoever, but only common Egypto-Phoenician motifs — motifs common on inscribed Hebrew seals as well. The excavators suggested that these bullae were from the royal archive of Samaria.[148]

In the Introduction, we mentioned the group of 17 Hebrew bullae discovered in a pottery juglet at Lachish. These had originally sealed letters and, after the opening of the papyri, the bullae were removed and placed in the juglet for safekeeping. The more recent group of 50 Hebrew bullae discovered in the City of David, contemporary with our assemblage, is further evidence of the common use of seals bearing private names in the sealing of documents in Judah. These bullae, generally similar to ours though lacking any official titles, have contributed little additional data concerning the character and functioning of archives of this sort.

After the destruction of the Kingdom of Judah, during the period of the Return from Exile (the Persian period), the use of bullae to seal documents continued in Judah, as shown by the discovery of 70 bullae bearing early Aramaic script noted in the Introduction. These bullae mention, *inter alia*, the province of "Yehud" and names of officials, and include an impression of one of the governors (ʾElnatan) and the seal of his maidservant, Shelomit. The composition of that find, and especially the fact that the bullae were accompanied by an actual seal of the province of "Yehud", leads to the assumption that that assemblage is to be associated with an official archive of Judah.[149] There, too, no documents were preserved, and nothing of their contents is known.

For lack of comparative material from the period of the Judean monarchy, we are forced to turn to later finds which comprise the desired combination of bullae and papyri. The largest and most important discovery of this type comes from the Jewish military colony at Elephantine in Upper Egypt, where numerous Aramaic papyri of the Persian period (5th–4th century BCE) were discovered.[150] These were administrative and legal documents, including letters, deeds of sale, marriage deeds, documents concerning finances and the like. The papyri had been folded several

148 Crowfoot & Crowfoot, *op. cit.* (above, n. 16), pp. 2, 88; Pl. 15: 29–30.

149 Avigad 1976a, p. 30; J. Naveh & J. C. Greenfield: "Hebrew and Aramaic in the Persian Period", in W. D. Davies & L. Finkelstein (eds.): *The Cambridge History of Judaism* I: *Introduction. The Persian Period*, Cambridge 1984, pp. 115–130, especially pp. 123–124, opine that it was the private archive of the maidservant Shelomit, and not an official archive. They also claim that ʾElnatan *pḥwʾ* did not hold the rank of governor, but was one of the "lower government officials". But it is unlikely that the maidservant of an ordinary official would have had such a formal seal, inscribed as "(Belonging) to Shelomit maidservant of ʾElnatan the *pḥwʾ*" and would have possessed such a large private archive. Further, how can the presence in a private archive of not only *yhd* bullae but even an actual *yhd* seal be explained?

150 E. Sachau: *Aramäische Papyrus aus einer jüdischen Militärkolonie zu Elephantine*, Leipzig 1911; E. G. Kraeling: *The Brooklyn Museum Aramaic Papyri*, New Haven 1953.

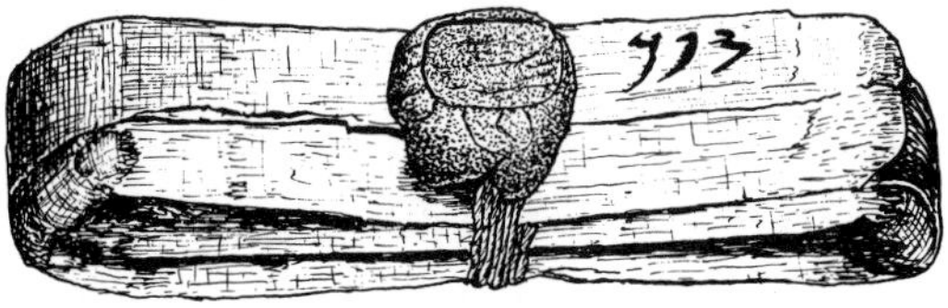

Fig. 1. Papyrus contract from Elephantine, sealed with a single bulla. On the papyrus, the word *spr* ("deed") is written in ink (after E. G. Kraeling).

Fig. 2. Samaria Papyrus 1, from Wadi Daliyeh, before unrolling, with its seven bullae still in place (after F.M. Cross).

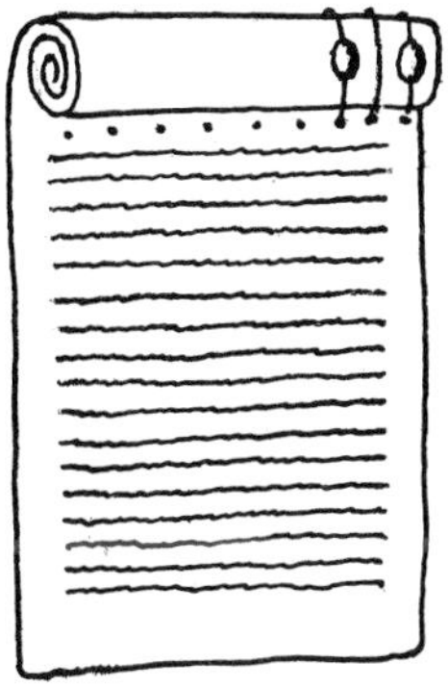

Fig. 3. A "double" deed from Avroman (after E. H. Minns).

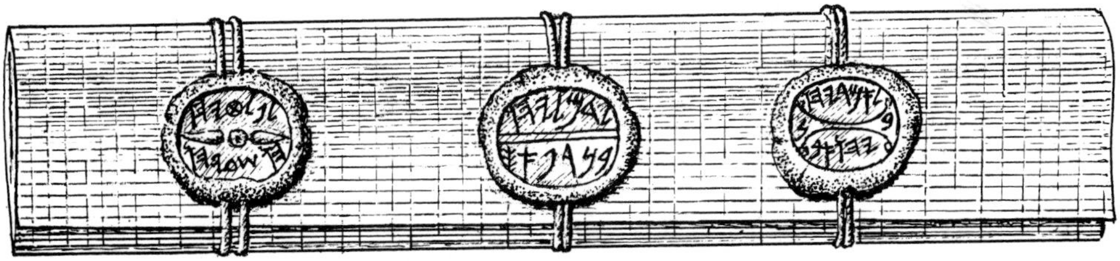

Fig. 4. Conjectural reconstruction of a "sealed deed" from the period of the Judean monarchy. Such a deed would seem to be referred to in Isaiah 29: 11: "... a book that is sealed. When men give it to one who can read, saying, 'Read this,' he says, 'I cannot, for it is sealed.'"

times and tied with string, which was then sealed with a single bulla stamped with an anepigraphic seal (see Fig. 1).

Another significant find came to light in 1962, in a cave in Wadi Daliyeh north of Jericho.[151] This cave served as a refuge for wealthy persons from Samaria who had fled before the approaching army of Alexander the Great. They brought with them legal documents written in Aramaic, dated to the end of the Persian period (second half of the 4th century BCE). The papyri, mostly in a poor state of preservation, were sealed with bullae, of which 128 were recovered. Each document was sealed with several bullae, and one was tied with string to which were still attached seven bullae in good condition (see Fig. 2). This, then, was the very type of document which would be kept sealed with its bullae intact, and only when some legal necessity arose would it be unsealed. The bullae bore ornamental motifs from the Greco-Persian repertory. Only two of the bullae were inscribed, in the palaeo-Hebrew script. F. M. Cross has opined that in the Persian period only officials possessed seals bearing private names. These Documents state that they were drawn up and sealed in the presence of high officials; indeed one of them, a deed of sale, was sealed with the seal of "[Yeshaᶜ]yahu son of [San]ballaṭ, Governor of Samaria.[152]

Another very interesting example of the use of bullae came to light in 1909, at Avroman in remote Kurdistan.[153] There a stone jar was found containing several documents on parchment, rolled up, tied and sealed with bullae. Three of them have survived. Dated to the 3rd century BCE, two documents are in Greek and one in Aramaic script. They were written and sealed in the following manner: the text was written twice, once, an "original" in the upper part of the page, and the second time in a "copy" in the lower part of the page, with a space in between; the upper part was then rolled up and bound with a string which was passed through small holes punched through the blank strip between the two texts. Lumps of clay were pressed over the strings and then impressed with the seals of all the parties to the contract. The lower text, which remained open for inspection at any time, was not sealed (see Fig. 3). These Avroman documents are a rare example of the survival of a "double document", half of which is sealed with bullae and the other half of which remains unsealed. In Latin, the closed, rolled-up portion was known as *scriptura interior*, while the open portion was known as *scriptura exterior*. If the open version was contested, the sealed version could be opened for verification in the presence of the authorities.

This practice of "double documents" (or "tied deeds" in the terminology of the Talmud) was well known in antiquity and was very common in Hellenistic times

151 F. M. Cross: "The Papyri and their Historical Implications", in P. W. Lapp & N. L. Lapp (eds.): *Discoveries in the Wadi ed-Daliyeh* (*Annual of the American Schools of Oriental Research* 41), New Haven 1974, p. 19.

152 *Ibid.*, Pl. 61.

153 E. H. Minns: "Parchments of the Parthian Period from Avroman", *Journal of Hellenic Studies* 35 (1915), pp. 22ff.

throughout the Seleucid and Ptolemaic domains.[154] But only in a few instances have such documents survived together with their bullae.[155] We may note one find from Egypt, reminiscent of the circumstances surrounding our bullae: 330 clay bullae purchased from a Cairo antiquities dealer in 1906 were stated to have been discovered in a large jar at Edfu.[156] On the backs of these bullae there were impressed traces of papyrus fibres, and on the front were symbols and figures in Greco-Egyptian style, but no script *per se*.

There are many examples of double documents from the Roman period, generally not sealed with bullae but rather by true signatures. First to come to mind are the numerous documents of the 2nd century CE from the family archive of Babata of En-Gedi, discovered in a cave in the Judean Desert.[157] From the same period is another group of bullae found in the Nabatean cemetery at Kurnub (Mampsis) in the Negev.[158] These 24 bullae were impressed with official seals of Nabatean cities. They bear symbols of the zodiac and all include Greek inscriptions giving the name of the city and the month of sealing. None of them bears a private name.

All these examples of the mode of sealing documents, and of the character of their contents, are of course later than our assemblage of bullae. In general it is wise to avoid projecting later practices back in time, but in this instance the many features are similar in the different periods — including utilization of the same two materials, papyrus and clay, which largely determined the procedures involved in drawing up the documents.

To round out our discussion, however, we must turn to the literary sources. The most illuminating description of the preparation of a deed of sale in the days of the Judean monarchy is found in the Bible; it concerns the purchase of a field by the Prophet Jeremiah at a time when he was incarcerated by the king. The relevance of the passage justifies the quotation of Jeremiah's own words (RSV, Jeremiah 32: 9–15):

> And I bought the field at Anathoth from Hanamel my cousin, and weighed out the money to him, seventeen shekels of silver. I signed the deed (*sepher*), sealed it, got witnesses, and weighed the money on scales. Then I took the sealed deed of purchase (*sepher hammiqnah*), containing the terms and conditions, and the open deed and I gave the deed of purchase to Baruch the son of Neriah son of Mahseiah, in the presence

154 For a comprehensive discussion of bullae in this context, see L. Wenger, in Pauly-Wissowa's *Realencyclopädie der Klassischen Altertumswissenschaft* 2/4, Stuttgart 1923, cols. 2361–2448, s.v. *Signum*.

155 M. Rostovtzeff: "Seleucid Babylonia — Bullae and Seals with Greek Inscriptions", *Yale Classical Studies* 3 (1932), pp. 1–114. These bullae are of a different form; the clay encircled the rolled document like a ring, stamped all around with the seals of the parties to the contract.

156 J. G. Milne: "Ptolemaic Seal Impressions", *Journal of Hellenic Studies* 36 (1916), pp. 87ff.

157 Y. Yadin: *Bar-Kokhba: The Rediscovery of the Legendary Hero* . . . ; London-Jerusalem 1971, pp. 222–253; for the tying of these documents, see pp. 229–231.

158 A. Negev: "Seal-Impressions from Tomb 107 at Kurnub (Mampsis)", *IEJ* 19 (1969), pp. 89–106.

> of Hanamel my cousin, in the presence of all the Jews who were sitting in the court of the guard. I charged Baruch in their presence, saying, "Thus says the Lord of hosts, the God of Israel: Take these deeds, both this sealed deed of purchase and this open deed, and put them in an earthenware vessel, that they may last for a long time. For thus says the Lord of hosts, the God of Israel: Houses and fields and vineyards shall again be bought in this land."

Though Jeremiah's purchase was of symbolic nature, as is evident from the final verse, this is most likely an accurate description of the legal procedure by which land sales were effected at that time. The "deed of purchase" (*sepher hammiqnah*), probably written on papyrus (as indicated, *inter alia*, by our bullae), was in this case sealed only with the seal of the purchaser. The witnesses apparently certified their testimony solely with their signatures in ink. It may be assumed that the seller too would sign the deed, but Jeremiah makes no mention of this. The first deed was termed the "sealed deed" because it was rolled up and sealed with a bulla or bullae; it contained the original version of the contract, and would be opened before the judicial authorities only when absolutely necessary — that is, when doubts arose concerning interpretation of the text. The second, "open deed" was a copy of the sealed, binding version, and was intended for normal perusal. Thus, there were definitely two texts, original and duplicate copy, written on two separate sheets of papyrus. Both were given to Baruch the scribe, who was present at the signing of the deed, for safekeeping.

The practice of writing contracts in two copies was very ancient. It is already known in early Mesopotamia, where the original cuneiform text was written on a clay tablet, with the copy written on a clay "envelope" enclosing the original. (However, in Jeremiah's day this practice was no longer current even in Mesopotamia.) The earliest mention of the writing of a contract in two copies on a pliable material (that is, on papyrus) is indeed the passage from the Book of Jeremiah quoted above. Material remains of such a document from the First Temple period have not been found.[159] The only archaeological evidence for "sealed deeds" in that period appears to be the bullae themselves, constituting as they did an integral part of rolled and sealed papyrus documents. (For a conjectural restoration of a sealed papyrus, see Fig. 4; the number of bullae affixed there, three, is arbitrary.)[160]

159 The bullae also constitute the principal evidence for the widespread use of papyrus in Palestine during the period of the Israelite Monarchy. So far, only a single fragment of a Hebrew papyrus of that period has come to light; see P. Benoit, J. T. Milik & R. de Vaux: *Les grottes de Murabbaʿat* (*Discoveries in the Judaean Desert* II), Oxford 1961, p. 96.

160 The number of bullae attached to a document in the pre-Exilic period remains uncertain. After our discussion of this problem, Professor Alan Millard, of the University of Liverpool, sent me a letter (dated 5 June 1985), from which I quote:

"I have tried to find examples of papyri with multiple sealings. So far, however, I have not seen reports of any from Egypt before the Greek period. Each of the hieratic papyri which survives with its cords and sealing intact bears only a single bulla. Recently, T. G. H. James of the British Museum gave a lecture here on seals in ancient Egypt, and he confirmed that

The careful storage of documents in the period of the First Temple is also illuminated by Jeremiah's words. Jeremiah told Baruch the scribe to place both versions of his deed of purchase, open and sealed, in a pottery jar, "that they may last for a long time". Indeed, archaeological discoveries have shown that this was a common method of storing documents and scrolls in antiquity.[161] Our bullae were most probably also found within pottery vessels, though such jars could have been broken during the fire which destroyed the papyri, and their sherds may well have been ignored by the discoverers of the bullae.

What did Baruch do with the vessel containing Jeremiah's deeds? How did he safeguard the documents placed in his custody? At his home? In an archive? This question cannot be decided. The owners of the Samaria Papyri had kept them at home, and when they fled to the cave in Wadi Daliyeh, they took the documents with them. Similarly, Babata of En-Gedi took 35 documents with her to the "Cave of Letters" when she fled the approaching Romans (most of hers were "tied deeds", though lacking bullae). The large number of documents pertaining directly to Babata's family indicates that they represent a family archive. In contrast, this does not seem to have been the case with our assemblage of bullae. As far as can be judged from the varied nature of the bullae, the documents they had sealed did not deal with a single family, but were much broader in scope. Thus, we would tend to regard this as the remnant of a public archive of some type — a sort of official chancery where administrative and legal documents were stored. It is impossible to prove this, however, for we lack actual, relevant evidence.

Another matter worthy of consideration is the true findspot of this archive. The most suitable location would be Jerusalem, for all the high officials who had sealed bullae in the assemblage surely resided at the capital of the kingdom. Josephus Flavius mentions an archive for documents and deeds, located in his day adjacent to the Temple Mount on the west. During the war against the Romans, the Jewish

Egyptian documents carry only one bulla each. Some are briefly described in J. Černý, *Late Ramesside Letters*, Brussels (1939), pp. xix, xx, and, so far as I can discover, all the others he mentioned there were similar. When the Germans excavated at Elephantine they recovered papyri of the fourth or third centuries B.C., in Greek, still tied with cords and bearing three bullae, with more than one impression on each (O. Rubensohn, *Elephantine Papyri, Sonderheft zu Berliner Griechische Urkunden*, Berlin, 1907; one is reproduced, I think, in W. Schubart, *Einführung in die Papyruskunde*, Berlin, 1918, Taf. IV.13). The Wadi Daliyeh example displayed in the Israel Museum has even more! I wonder if this multiple sealing is a late innovation, for, although cuneiform tablets of the second millennium B.C. often bear several seal impressions, those of the neo-Assyrian period usually have only one. J. N. Postgate, *Fifty Neo-Assyrian Legal Deeds*, Warminster, 1976, says 'only the man whose consent was needed [for the transaction] would impress his seal ...', he would be the seller of a property, or the borrower of a loan. Of course, in Jeremiah 32 it is the purchaser who seals the deed. So whether the three hundred odd bullae did belong to three hundred odd separate documents, or whether they belonged to a much smaller number will have to remain uncertain. Perhaps the balance of probability is in favour of one bulla for each deed."

I wish to thank Professor Millard for these interesting comments.

161 Some of the Qumran Scrolls were discovered within jars.

zealots burnt it to the ground, so as to destroy all the "promissory notes" of the debtors and thereby bring the collection of moneys to a standstill.[162] In the period of the First Temple, too, there was probably an archive adjacent to the Temple, as at many temples of the ancient world.

But the antiquities dealers stated that the bullae were not found in Jerusalem. As we have noted, it is not always possible to rely on their testimony. It has been surmised orally that the archive was transferred in antiquity, for some unknown reason, from Jerusalem to one of the outlying towns of the kingdom. Another theory holds that our assemblage of bullae actually came to light in illicit excavations in Jerusalem (that is, in the City of David). This possibility cannot be rejected out of hand, but it is nevertheless doubtful because of the timing and circumstances of the appearance of the find on the antiquities market. Indeed, the current City of David excavations were not yet in progress, and any considerable activity on the site could hardly have passed unnoticed.

In any event, I think we must not eliminate the possibility of a public archive or official chancery existing even at some district seat in Judah, operating in conjunction with high officials in the capital. Administrative ties of this sort between capital and outlying towns would be indicated by such bullae as those of "Gedalyahu who is over the house" and "Shebanyahu [son of] the king" discovered at Lachish, and the bulla of "Geʾalyahu son of the king" found at Beth-Zur (as well as among our bullae). But this does not exclude the possibility that some of these ministers had duplicate seals for use in outlying towns. The available data are too sparse to allow a fuller discussion of this matter and we should, therefore, leave its solution to future evidence and imagination.

One fact, however, is quite certain: the identification of the owner of the bulla inscribed "Berekhyahu son of Neriyahu the scribe" (No. 9) with Baruch the son of Neriah the scribe, who was an eye-witness to the symbolic-historical event of the purchase of a field by Jeremiah, and into whose hands the prophet placed his deeds for safekeeping. It can be assumed that this Baruch was no passive onlooker at the signing of the contract, but served as the scribe drawing up the document, and perhaps even sealed it with his seal (although this is not stated in the biblical account). His seal-impression there would presumably have been similar to that in our assemblage, which bears his name and title.

As noted, a bulla of Yeraḥmeʾel son of the king was found together with that of Berekhyahu the scribe, and Yeraḥmeʾel appears also to have been connected with the above events. This, indeed, is a most unusual occurrence — we have before us objects bearing the names of their owners, persons who can be identified with certainty with two high-ranking biblical officials in a single, known episode. This in itself lends our assemblage of bullae special value as historical and chronological documents of the first order.

Our quest for the identity of those two seal-owners has led us to one of the most fascinating episodes in the Book of Jeremiah — chapters 32 and, especially, 36

162 Josephus Flavius: *The Jewish War* II, 17, 6.

where we find for the first time mention of Baruch the son of Neriah the son of Mahseiah, the scribe — the secretary, confidant and recorder of the life and prophecies of the Prophet Jeremiah. The time was the period of Jeremiah's struggle against the treaty between Judah and Egypt, which was directed against Babylon.[163] He saw in the opposition to Babylon a danger to the very existence of the Kingdom of Judah. In this context, Jeremiah found a loyal assistant in Baruch the scribe.

In the fourth year of King Jehoiakim of Judah (605/604 BCE), Baruch set down in a scroll, from dictation, the words of Jeremiah — the prophecies against the nations, including that on the destruction of Judah and Jerusalem. A year later, in King Jehoiakim's fifth year, Baruch read out these prophecies before the people at the chamber of Gemariah the son of Shaphan the scribe,[164] in the Upper Court of the Temple. Later, he again read them out before the council of ministers meeting at the chamber of Elishama the scribe, which was at the King's House. Finally, when the scroll was read out before the king himself, he became filled with wrath and he burnt the scroll, ordering both Jeremiah and Baruch to be arrested. This task was given to Jerahmeel the son of the king (the owner of the seal of the other bulla, No. 8) and to two other officials (Jeremiah 36: 26). Forewarned, Baruch and Jeremiah hid, and Jeremiah instructed the scribe to rewrite the scroll, adding further prophecies on the harsh punishment to be meted out to the king for his destruction of the first scroll.

163 See A. Malamat: "The Twilight of Judah: In the Egyptian-Babylonian Maelstrom", *Vetus Testamentum, Supplement* 28 (1974), pp. 123–145.

164 Among the bullae recently discovered in the City of David (see Shiloh 1984 and 1985), there is one inscribed *lgmryhw bn špn*. Y. Shiloh suggests that this person should be identified with Gemaryahu the son of Shaphan the scribe (Jeremiah 36: 10), assuming that this Gemaryahu was a scribe of King Jehoiakim. But we may note that it is very unlikely that a royal scribe would omit his title from his own seal. Furthermore, it is doubtful whether Gemaryahu was a scribe at all. Many scholars and commentators consider rather that he was the son of Shaphan the scribe, who served under Josiah. The royal scribe under Jehoiakim was Elishama the scribe, in whose bureau at the king's palace Baruch read out Jeremiah's scroll for the second time, before the ministers. On that occasion, all the ministers were present: "Elishama the scribe (*sopher*), Delaiah the son of Shemaiah, Elnathan the son of Achbor, Gemariah the son of Shaphan, Zedekiah the son of Hananiah, and all the princes (*śarim*)" (Jeremiah 36: 12). Note that Elishama is listed first, and that he is denoted scribe, while Gemariah is mentioned among the other officials without a specific title. He had a bureau at the Temple, as did other such officials.

Some of the more recent opinions on this matter are as follows: Mettinger (*op. cit.*, n. 5, pp. 31–34) holds that there is no evidence that Gemaryahu inherited the office of scribe from his father, Shaphan, although such a possibility does exist. De Vaux (*op. cit.*, above, n. 5, p. 131) mentions among the scribes only Elishama, and ignores Gemaryahu altogether. Bright claims that Gemaryahu was the son of Shaphan the scribe, but was not himself a scribe (see J. Bright: *Jeremiah* [*The Anchor Bible*], Garden City, New Jersey, 1963, p. 180). In most of the encyclopaedias, Gemaryahu is defined as the son of Shaphan the scribe, and not as a scribe himself. In the Hebrew *Enṣ. Miqr.* V, s.v. *sopher* (by A. F. Rainey), Gemaryahu is not mentioned among the scribes of that period; but in the entry on *peqidut* ("Bureaucracy" — by S. Yeivin), Gemaryahu is included in the list of scribes.

Baruch the son of Neriah loyally stood beside Jeremiah throughout this stormy period, and continued to serve him even after the prophet had been cast into prison by King Zedekiah, in the midst of Nebuchadnezzar's siege of Jerusalem (Jeremiah 32: 3–4). After the Babylonian conquest, and after the murder at Mizpah of Gedaliah the son of Ahikam who was appointed Governor of Judah by the King of Babylon, a group of refugees carried Jeremiah and Baruch to Egypt, much against their will (Jeremiah 43: 6). In these episodes we see Baruch the scribe as an exalted figure who took a significant part in the life and deeds of Jeremiah. Many scholars consider that he was Jeremiah's Boswell, and that his writings served as the basis for the Book of Jeremiah.[165]

We know very little about Jeraḥmeel son of the king. From what is stated in Jeremiah 36: 26, his office was connected with "police" activities, such as the arrest of opponents of the king. As a member of the royal family in official service he also fulfilled other functions, as can be seen from his bulla in our assemblage. The bullae of Baruch/Berekhyahu and Yeraḥme'el were impressed by their owners in their administrative or legal capacities. It is reasonable to assume that, since the bulla of Berekhyahu was found together with a large group of bullae of other high officials, Baruch/Berekhyahu was acting within the same official framework in which the other officials were operating.

This raises the question, controversial among scholars, concerning the status of Baruch the scribe: was he an official scribe, or only Jeremiah's personal scribe? The latter view enjoys greater favour among scholars, for Baruch is mentioned only in connection with Jeremiah. But it is not necessarily correct. The discovery of a bulla impressed by Berekhyahu among the bullae of royal officials would seem to indicate that at the time of its sealing Baruch was serving as an official scribe. He was of a noble family, and his brother, Seriah the son of Neriah, was a minister at Zedekiah's court and was sent to Babylon on an important mission (Jeremiah 59: 64).[166] Baruch seems eventually to have left his official position and joined Jeremiah in his struggle against the pro-Egyptian, anti-Babylonian policy of the court, a policy which was soon to lead to the destruction of Jerusalem.

If Baruch had previously been a scribe in royal service, then it might be assumed that the bulla bearing his name reached the archive (along with its document) at a time when Baruch was still an official; that is, prior to 605/604 BCE, when he wrote out Jeremiah's scroll. In any event, the ascription of the two impressions of the seals of Berekhyahu and Yeraḥme'el to the very end of the 7th century BCE — that is, to the end of the Judean monarchy — is certain. The archive probably continued in use for another eighteen years, until it was burned upon the fall of Judah in 586 BCE.

165 J. Muilenberg: "Baruch the Scribe", in J. I. Durham & J. R. Porter (eds.): *Proclamation and Presence, Old Testament Essays in Honor of* G. H. *Davies*, London 1970, pp. 215–238.

166 See Avigad 1978b; Avigad 1978a, p. 56.

LIST OF ABBREVIATIONS

Arad Inscriptions	Y. Aharoni: *Arad Inscriptions*, Jerusalem 1975 (Hebrew); 1981 (English)
Avigad 1953	N. Avigad, "On Two 'Aḥab' Stamps", *BIES* 17, pp. 47–48 (Hebrew)
Avigad 1954	N. Avigad, "Seven Ancient Hebrew Seals", *BIES* 18, pp. 147–153 (Hebrew)
Avigad 1963	N. Avigad, "Two Newly Found Hebrew Seals", *IEJ* 13, pp. 322–324
Avigad 1964	N. Avigad, "Seals and Sealings", *IEJ* 14, pp. 190–194
Avigad 1966	N. Avigad, "A Hebrew Seal with a Family Emblem", *IEJ* 16, pp. 50–53
Avigad 1968	N. Avigad, "The Seal of Abigad", *IEJ* 18, pp. 52–53
Avigad 1969	N. Avigad, "A Group of Hebrew Seals", *EI* 9 (Albright Volume), pp.1–9, Pls. א-ג (Hebrew; English summary on p. 134)
Avigad 1970	N. Avigad, "Ammonite and Moabite Seals", in J. A. Sanders, ed.: *Near Eastern Archaeology in the Twentieth Century. Essays in Honor of N. Glueck*, New York, pp. 284–294
Avigad 1975	N. Avigad, "New Names on Hebrew Seals", *EI* 12 (Glueck Volume), pp. 66–71, Pl. יד (Hebrew; English summary on pp. 120*–121*)
Avigad 1976a	N. Avigad: *Bullae and Seals from a Post-Exilic Judean Archive* (*Qedem* 4), Jerusalem
Avigad 1976b	N. Avigad, "The Governor of the City (śar haʿir)", *IEJ* 26, pp. 178–182
Avigad 1976c	N. Avigad, "New Light on the Naʿar-Seals", in F. M. Cross et al., eds.: *Magnalia Dei. The Mighty Acts of God. Essays on the Bible and Archaeology in Memory of G. Ernest Wright*, Garden City, N.Y., pp. 194–300
Avigad 1978a	N. Avigad, "Baruch the Scribe and Jerahmeel the King's Son", *IEJ* 28, pp. 52–56
Avigad 1978b	N. Avigad, "The Seal of Seraiah (son of) Neriah", *EL* 14 (Ginzberg Volume), pp. 86–87, Pl. נז (Hebrew; English summary on p. 125*)
Avigad 1979	N. Avigad, "A Group of Hebrew Seals from the Hecht Collection", *Festschrift Rëuben R. Hecht*, Jerusalem, pp. 119–126
Avigad 1981	N. Avigad, "Titles and Symbols on Hebrew Seals", *EI* 15 (Aharoni Volume), pp. 303–305, Pl. 1:3 (Hebrew; English summary on p. 85*)
Avigad 1982	N. Avigad, "A Hebrew Seal Depicting a Sailing Ship", *BASOR* 246, pp. 59-62
BASOR	*Bulletin of the American Schools of Oriental Research*
BIES	*Bulletin of the Israel Exploration Society* (Hebrew)
Bordreuil-Lemaire 1976	P. Bordreuil & A. Lemaire, "Nouveaux sceaux hébreux, araméens et ammonites", *Semitica* 26, pp. 45–63, Pls. IV–VI
Bordreuil-Lemaire 1982	P. Bordreuil & A. Lemaire, "Nouveaux sceaux hébreux et araméens", *Semitica* 32, pp. 21–34, Pls. V–VI
Cowley	A. Cowley: *Aramaic Papyri of the Fifth Century B.C.*, Oxford 1923
Diringer	D. Diringer: *Le iscrizioni antico-ebraiche palestinesi*, Florence 1934
EI	*Eretz-Israel. Archaeological, Historical and Geographical Studies* (Hebrew)
Enṣ. Miqr.	*Enṣiqlopediya Miqra'it (Encyclopaedia Biblica)*, Jerusalem 1950–1982 (Hebrew)
Hestrin-Dayagi	R. Hestrin & M. Dayagi-Mendels: *Inscribed Seals, First Temple Period. Hebrew, Ammonite, Moabite, Phoenician and Aramaic. From the Collections of the Israel Museum and the Israel Department of Antiquities and Museums*, Jerusalem 1979
IEJ	*Israel Exploration Journal*
Lachish Letters	H. Torczyner: *The Lachish Letters* (*Lachish* I), London 1938; N. H. Torczyner: *Te'udot Lakhish*, Jerusalem 1940 (Hebrew)
Moscati	S. Moscati: *L'epigrafia ebraica antica 1935–1950*, Rome 1951

Noth	M. Noth: *Die israelitischen Personennamen in Rahmen der gemeinsemitischen Namengebung*, Stuttgart 1928
Shiloh 1984	Y. Shiloh: *Excavations in the City of David 1978–1982* (*Qedem* 19), Jerusalem
Shiloh 1985	Y. Shiloh, "A Hoard of Hebrew Bullae from the City of David", *EI* 18 (Avigad Volume), pp. 73–87 (Hebrew; English summary on p. 68*)
Tallqvist	K. L. Tallqvist: *Assyrian Personal Names*, Helsinki 1914
Vattioni 1969	F. Vattioni, "I sigilli ebraica", *Biblica* 50, pp. 357–388
Vattioni 1971	F. Vattioni, "I sigilli ebraica II", *Augustinianum* 11, pp. 447–454
Vattioni 1978	F. Vattioni, "Sigilli ebraici III", *Annali dell'Istituto Universitario Orientale di Napoli* 38, pp. 227–254

INDEX OF NAMES AND TITLES

The numbers refer to seal/bulla numbers, while the letters refer to duplicate impressions. Paired numbers (e.g. 20–21) and + imply items ascribed to the same individual; * denotes a name or form not appearing in the Bible. In the English, names in parentheses are the forms in the Revised Standard Version of the English Bible.

A. Hebrew: Names

[א]ביהו — 13
אדניהו — 1+2 א-ב, 11, 125, 165
* [א]דניחי — 113
אחאב — 16, 17+18 א-ג, 19, 60
* אחאמה — 151
אחיהו — 13, 166
אחמלך — 129
אחקם — 14, 15, 16
אליהו — 27, 85
* אליסמך — 39
* אליעז — 28, 71
* אלירם — 29
אלנתן — 30
* אלסמך — 40
* אלעז — 17+18 א-ג, 72-73, 90
* [א]לצד[ק] — 84
אלשמע — 4, 66, 158-160
אמריהו — 31 א-ב
* אפרח — 19, 20-21, 22-23
אשחר — 32
* אשיהו — 33, 105 א-ב, 110
* אשרחי — 34, 126 א-יד
* [א]שריחת — 127

בניהו — 35
* בעדיהו — 36, 37
ברכיהו — 9, 38

* גאליהו — 6
גדי — 25 א-ב
* גדיהו — 23+24 א-ד, 26, 169
גדליהו — 5, 41
* געלי — 39, 40

* דמליהו — 42 א-ג, 43-46, 170

הודויהו — 55, 117
הושעיהו — 28, 41, 43 א-ב+44-46, 47 א-ב,
48, 143-145 א-ב+146-148, 161

* הצליהו — 49 א-ב, 128, 168

זכר — 50, 51
זרח — 62

* חבא — 52
חגב — 53-54 א-ב
חגי — 55
חטש — 56 א-ג
חלץ — 60, 142
* חלציהו — 47 א-ב, 79, 157
חלק — 57, 98, 149
חלקיהו — 58, 59, 107
* חמל — 83
חנן — 63, 64
חנני — 150
חנניהו — 61, 62, 100

טביהו — 14, 65

* יאזן — 162
* יאש — 30, 66, 67
ידעיהו — 68 א-ב, 69
יהוא — 70
יהואב — 31 א-ב
* יהואח — 71-73
* יהוזרח — 118
* יהועז — 74
* יהוקם — 12, 171
יהושע — 20, 21
* יסף — 131
יקמיהו — 11, 75, 76 א-ג, 77, 172
ירחמאל — 8
ירמ[יהו] — 78
ישמעאל — 78, 79, 80, 81, 82, 89, 101-102,
164, 173
ישעיהו — 83, 84, 91

* כסלא — 132

Titles

B. English: Names

Titles

LIST OF BULLA INSCRIPTIONS

The names in this list appear in complete form, even where they have been restored. The numbers refer to seal/bulla numbers, whereas the letters refer to duplicate impressions. Unmarked numbers represent bullae in the Yoav Sasson Collection; starred numbers represent bullae at the Israel Museum; the numbers marked ° remain in the hands of antiquities dealers.

1	לאדניהו אשר על הבית	(Seal 1)
2a	לאדניהו אשר על הבית	(Seal 2)
2b	לאדניהו אשר על הבית	(Seal 2)
*3	לנתן אשר על הבית	
4	לאלשמע עבד המלך	
5	לגדליהו עבד המלך	
*6	לגאליהו בן המלך	
7	לנריהו בן המלך	
8	לירחמאל בן המלך	
*9	לברכיהו בן נריהו הספר	
10	שר הער	
11	לאדניהו בן יקמיהו	(left frag.)
*11	לאדניהו בן יקמיהו	(right frag.)
12	לפדיהו / יהוקם	
°13	לאחיהו / אביהו	
*14	לאחקם בן טביהו	
15	לאחקם / נריהו	
16	אחקם / אחאב	
17	לאלעז בן אחאב	(Seal 1)
18a	לאלעז בן אחאב	(Seal 2)
18b	לאלעז בן אחאב	(Seal 2)
18c	לאלעז בן אחאב	(Seal 2)
19	לאחאב בן אפרח	
20	לאפרח בן יהושע	(Seal 1)
°21	לאפרח בן יהושע בן מתניהו	(Seal 2)
22	לאפרח בן שחר	(Seal 1)
*23	לאפרח בן שחר בן גדיהו	(Seal 2)
*23a	לשחר בן גדיהו	(Seal 1)
24b	לשחר בן גדיהו	(Seal 1)
*24c	לשחר בן גדיהו	(Seal 1)
*24d	לשחר בן גדיהו	(Seal 1)
*25a	לשחר בן גדיהו	(Seal 2)
25b	לשחר בן גדיהו	(Seal 2)
*26	לשחר בן גדיהו	(Seal 3)
*27	לאליהו בן מיכה	
28	לאליעז בן הושעיהו	
°29	לאלירם / שמעיהו	
30	לאלנתן בן יאש	
*31a	לאמריהו בן יהואב	
31b	לאמריהו בן יהואב	
32	לאשחר בן עשיהו	
33	לאשיהו בן שמעיהו	
34	לאשרחי / עשיהו	
35	בניהו / עליהו	
36	לבעדיהו ...	
37	לבעדיהו / שריהו	
38	לברכיהו בן שמעיהו	(lower frag.)
*38	לברכיהו בן שמעיהו	(upper frag.)
39	לגעלי בן אליסמך	(Seal 1)
40	לגעלי בן אלסמך	(Seal 2)
41a	לגדליהו / הושעיהו	(right frag.)
*41b	לגדליהו / הושעיהו	(left frag.)
42a	לדמליהו בן רפא	
42b	לדמליהו בן רפא	
*42c	לדמליהו בן רפא	
*43a	לדמליהו בן הושעיהו	(Seal 1)
43b	לדמליהו בן הושעיהו	(Seal 1)
44	לדמליהו בן הושעיהו	(Seal 2)
45	לדמליהו בן הושעיהו	(Seal 3)
46	לדמליהו / הושעיהו	(Seal 4)
47a	להושעיהו / חלציהו	
*47b	להושעיהו / חלציהו	
48	להושעיהו / שמע	
49 a	להצליהו בן שבניהו	
49b	להצליהו בן שבניהו	
50	לזכר בן נריהו	
51	לזכר בן ...יהו	
52	לחבא בן מתן	
53a	לחגב בן צפניהו	(Seal 1)
53b	לחגב בן צפניהו	(Seal 1)
*54a	לחגב בן צפניהו	(Seal 2)
*54b	לחגב בן צפניהו	(Seal 2)
55	לחגי בן הודויהו	
56a	לחטש / בן שפטיהו	
56b	לחטש / בן שפטיהו	
56c	לחטש / בן שפטיהו	
*57	לחלק בן עזר	
58	לחלקיהו בן ...יהו	
*59	לחלקיהו בן ...	
°60	לחלץ בן אחאב	

*61 לחנניהו / נחמיהו
62 חנניהו / זרח
63 לחנן בן עזריהו
64 לחנן בן שמעיהו
65 לטביהו / עבדא
66 ליאש בן אלשמע
67 ליאש בן פדיהו
°68a לידעיהו בן כרמי
68b לידעיהו בן כרמי
*69 לידעיהו בן שעל
70 ליהוא בן משמש
71 ליהואח / אליעז (Seal 1)
72 ליהואח / אלעז (Seal 2)
°73 ליהואח בן אלעז (Seal 3)
74a יהועז בן מתן
74b יהועז בן מתן
75a ליקמיהו בן משלם
75b ליקמיהו בן משלם
75c ליקמיהו בן משלם
76 ליקמיהו ...
77 ליקמיהו בן נחם
78 לירמיהו / ישמעאל
79 לישמעאל בן שעל בן חלציהו
80 לישמעאל בן מחסיהו
81 לישמעאל בן ...
82 לישמעאל ...
*83 לישעיהו בן חמל
84 לישעיהו בן אלצדק
85 למחסיהו / אליהו
86 למחסיהו בן פלטיהו
*87 למעשיהו / מיאמן
88 למיאמן בן עפי
*89 למירב / ישמעאל
90 למכיהו בן אלעז
91 למכיהו / ישעיהו
92 למכיהו בן משלם
93 לסמכיהו בן עמדיהו
94 למכיהו / פלטיהו
95 למכיהו בן שחר
96 למכיהו / שבניהו (Seal 1)
97 למכיהו / שבניהו (Seal 2)
*98 למלכיהו / חלק
99 למלכיהו בן פדיהו
*100 למנחם / חנניהו
101 למנחם בן ישמעאל (Seal 1)
102 למנחם בן ישמעאל (Seal 2)
103 למנחם בן מנש
104 למנחם / פגי
105a למעשיהו / אשיהו
*105b למעשיהו / אשיהו
106 למספר בן ...
107 למעשיהו / חלקיהו
108 מצר בן שלם
109 למקנמלך ...
110 למשלם / אשיהו
111 למשלם בן רפאיהו
112 למשען בן שחר
113 למתן בן אדניחי בן שחר
°114 למתן בן פלטיהו (Seal 1)
115 למתן בן פלטיהו (Seal 2)
°116a למתן בן פלטיהו (Seal 3)
116b למתן בן פלטיהו (Seal 3)
117 למתן בן הודויהו
118 למתן בן יהוזרח
119 למתניהו בן סמכיהו
*120 לנגבי בן מלכיהו
121 לנחם בן רפאיהו
*122 לנמש בן נריהו
123 לנמשר בן שעל
124 לנמשר בן שבניהו
125 לנריהו / אדניהו
126a לנריהו / אשרחי
126b לנריהו / אשרחי
126c לנריהו / אשרחי
126d לנריהו / אשרחי
126e לנריהו / אשרחי
126f לנריהו / אשרחי
126g לנריהו / אשרחי
126h לנריהו / אשרחי
126i לנריהו / אשרחי
°126j לנריהו / אשרחי
126k לנריהו / אשרחי
126l לנריהו / אשרחי
126m לנריהו / אשרחי
126n לנריהו / אשרחי
°127 לנריהו / אשריחת
128 לנריהו בן הצליהו
*129 לנתן / אחמלך
*130 לנתן / פדיהו
*131 לסאל בן יסף
132 לסלא בן כסלא
133a לסעדיהו בן ...
133b לסעדיהו בן ...
134 לעבדיהו בן נתן
135a לעזר / פלטיהו
*135b לעזר / פלטיהו
°136 לעזריהו בן ס[מך]
137 לעזריהו בן פדיהו
138a לעזרקם בן פרפר
138b לעזרקם בן פרפר
139 לעזרקם בן צדקא
140 לעבבר ...
141 לעליהו / רפא
142 לעליהו / חלץ

143a	לפלטיהו בן הושעיהו (Seal 1)
143b	לפלטיהו בן הושעיהו (Seal 1)
144a	לפלטיהו / הושעיהו (Seal 2)
144b	לפלטיהו / הושעיהו (Seal 2)
145a	לפלטיהו / הושעיהו (Seal 3)
145b	לפלטיהו / הושעיהו (Seal 3)
146	לפלטיהו / ... (Seal 4)
°147	לפלטיהו / הושעיהו (Seal 5)
*148	לפלטיהו בן הושעיה (Seal 6)
*149	לפלטיהו בן חלק
150	לפנ... ב. / חנני
151	לפשחר בן אחאמה
*152	לפשחר בן מנחם
153	לפתח בן נחם
154	צפן / מקניהו
155	לצפניהו / שאלה
156	לקרבאר בן עזראל
157a	לראיהו / חלציהו
157b	לראיהו / חלציהו
*158	לשלם בן אלשמע (Seal 1)
159	לשלם בן אלשמע (Seal 2)
160	לשלם בן אלשמע (Seal 3)
161	לשלם בן הושעיהו
162	לישמעאל / יאזן
163	לשמעיהו / ...
164	לשעל בן ישמעאל
165	לשפטיהו / אדניהו
166	לשפט / אחיהו
167	לשבניהו / שריהו
168	לתנחם / הצליהו
169	... / בן / גדיהו
170	.... / דמליהו בן ...
*171	... / יהוקם
*172	... / יקמיהו
173	... / ישמעאל
174	לשעל בן מלכיהו
175	.... / מלכיהו
176	.... / בן נחם
177	.... / עזיהו
178	.... / פדיהו
179	....יהו / שמעיהו
180a	.... / בן שפטיהו
180b	.... / בן שפטיהו
*181	....מב / ....יאל
182	....שע / ...יהו
183	....יהו / [פש]חר
184	למ.... / בן....
185	....עיהו / ....שיהו
*186	....יהו / ...יהו
187	....יהו / ....ליהו
188	....ניהו / ....הו
*189	ליהו....
190	ליהו.... / ....עיה
191	...איהו / ....
192	....יהוד / ....ליהו
193	.... / ....יה.
*194	....יהו בן / ....עי....
195	....עמל.... / ....
196	לשל.... / ....
197	....ליהו /
198	....הו / ....ר
199	[אד]ניהו / ... (Scarab)
200	(Uraeus) ....ר....
*201	(Uraeus)
202	[נ]חם / [ש]בע (Bird)
203	זי.... (Quadruped)
204	(Quadruped)
205	(Tree)
206	(Palmette Capital)
207	Illegible
208	Illegible
209	Illegible
*210	Illegible
211	Illegible

DEC 14 1989	DATE DUE		
DEC 16 1988			
FEB 22 1992			
JAN 04 2007			
JAN 02 2007			